HOW TO CHOOSE AND ENJOY WINE

HOW TO CHOOSE
AND ENJOY WINE

EDITED BY
AUGUSTUS MUIR

With contributions by
H. WARNER ALLEN
JOHN BURGOYNE
IAN M. CAMPBELL
FREDERICK A. COCKBURN
STANLEY F. DAVIS
FREDERICK HENNESSY
ALFRED LANGENBACH
FREDERICK ROSSI
A. J. B. RUTHERFORD
ANDRÉ L. SIMON
CHARLES WILLIAMS

BONANZA BOOKS · NEW YORK

Decorations by Paul Hogarth

517RO1440

This edition published by Bonanza Books
a division of Crown Publishers, Inc.,
by arrangement with Hamlyn Publishing Group Limited

b

Manufactured in the United States of America

CONTENTS

CONTENTS

*The Editor has provided lists of Vintages and
Shippers at the end of the appropriate chapters.*

CHOOSING AND ENJOYING

BY AUGUSTUS MUIR

1. Invitation to Wine

OUR enjoyment of wine depends not only on a fine palate. The wine we drink must be well chosen to suit the occasion, the season of the year, the weather, the time of day, the food, the companion. To help the beginner who enjoys wine and would like to enjoy it more, I have asked a group of writers, whose names bear the seal of authority, to contribute to this book the best advice they can give. After studying their words, I hope the reader will find greater pleasure than before in drinking a sound, unpretentious *ordinaire*; and I hope, also, that he will find the gate thrown open to the deeper enjoyment that follows the cultivation of a sensitive palate.

I would ask you, first of all, to consider the difference between the drinking of wine and of beer. One takes beer with an open throat; one tastes it as one swallows it. "Quaff a tankard of ale"—the phrase exactly describes the business. Wine, on the contrary, must be taken into the mouth and held with the throat closed. The finer the wine the more deliberately, thoughtfully, it should be drunk.

Let us suppose you have been having a talk with your wine merchant, and he pours out a glass of Burgundy or red Bordeaux which he would like you to taste before he tells you its name or price. You are about to have a fascinating and exciting adventure with wine, and you are challenged to give your verdict.

2. A Problem in Detection

The colour is the first thing to examine. Hold the glass up to the light. Is there the faintest hint of cloudiness? You can tell this better at the edge of the glass than at the centre. A purple tinge in the red will indicate that the wine is young. A pale-brown tinge will suggest age—which need not necessarily be the result of years, for the wine may have grown old quickly. The next step is to savour the bouquet.

This should not be rushed. A strong trace of grape at the first sniff will suggest extreme youth. Some elements in the grape can survive the hot, tumultuous process of fermentation, and the grape-like smell of a very young wine may be stronger than the evaporating ethers and essences that arise from the wine itself. Perhaps the wine in your glass has already lost its "grape smell" and developed "wine smell"— that delicate mingling of odours which has inspired so many pages of glowing prose. If the wine has very little bouquet this must be considered a mark against it, for I assume it has been presented to you in a fair state—that is, not too cold nor with the cork newly drawn. Swirl the wine gently round to let the air mix with it. This may help the bouquet to make itself known.

And now for the tasting.

Some say: take only a very tiny sip; others recommend a

goodish mouthful. Anyhow, you will want enough to "get a grip" of the wine. Taste it fully and affectionately. "Chew your wine, my son, chew it!" is a well-known piece of old-fashioned advice from a French wine-taster. Let it flood over your tongue and under it—for one part of the tongue responds to sweetness, another to saltness. As the wine grows warm, draw in a little air over it and breathe down your nose, assessing the bouquet once more. Let the wine flow round your gums—the reason I will mention in a moment.

At last, having given your palate time to respond, swallow the wine and wait for the result. You are now experiencing the wine's "farewell"—its finish—which should be entirely pleasant and satisfying, a sensation of sweetness relieved and given "character" by just the faintest touch of astringency. The farewell can tell you much about a wine's quality—and can go a long way in helping an expert to locate the district where it was grown.

Consider now whether the combined effect is one of coarseness, sharpness, lack of "sugar." Or has it the good qualities of a sound wine—a bouquet without too prominent a suggestion of the grape, and at the same time a good body with some sweetness in it and a clean, pleasant farewell? Or has it, in very truth, got that subtle appeal, that finely balanced flavour, with an exquisite bouquet as its prelude, and a smooth suave farewell to round off your taste of a wine of high quality?

While you make up your mind about the experience you have just had, let me mention an important fact. Every time we speak of "taste" we are apt to forget that our sense of smell is a powerful assistant. The well-known "onion or apple" experiment will show what I mean. After a person's nose has been plugged and his eyes bandaged he is given a spoonful of mashed apple to taste, then one of mashed onion, and is invited to guess which is which. He may well find it hard to decide, for the *taste* of onion and apple can be surprisingly similar, and he feels lost without his sense of smell to guide him. How the taste of a wine is enriched by its perfume!

I mentioned the impact of the wine on one's gums. The result can now be noted. If there is a drawing together as from a contact with alum, it is fairly certain that the wine has too much tannin—Nature's preservative of all red wine. In the right proportion it helps to give character. A wine with too little will not hold together; on the other hand, too much of it makes for hardness and may delay the development of the wine in bottle. Nowadays, in many wine-growing areas, the wine is made deliberately with a low tannin content so that it will mature quickly and become softer on the palate.

3. Consider Your Verdict

And now has come the moment for you to give your verdict to the wine merchant. Whatever you have to say about Colour, Bouquet, Taste, Farewell, I am sure you will learn much from the discussion that will follow. Let me quickly add that the tests I have described can be carried out only in the privacy of the wine merchant's parlour or in your own home. The more dignified ritual recommended by Colonel Ian Campbell on a subsequent page is the one for the dining-room or restaurant. When one is tasting a number of wines, it is customary and wise to spit out what one has tasted: it would be unkind to the stomach to startle it with a succession of wines swallowed without food. Let me add, too, that the tests I have suggested can be modified to apply to any wine, red or white, still or sparkling, natural or fortified.

4. Tasting White Wines

In examining a white wine, note if the colour is a pale straw, a medium yellow, a golden yellow, or a yellow with a tinge of green. Some of the finest white wines have this hint of green—a *genuine* Chablis, for instance. If there is a tinge of brown you will suspect it of being past its best. The wine should be quite clear. To achieve complete transparency some are put through so sharp an asbestos filter that the marrow is taken out of them. If a brilliantly clear wine has poor body and lacks depth of flavour its substance may have been sacrificed for an artificial clarity to catch the buyer's eye.

The bouquet of a great Sauternes will be full and sometimes almost overpoweringly heavy with sweetness. That of a fine white Burgundy will be clean, fresh, smooth, while the finer Hocks and Moselles can have at their best a delicious bouquet with an almost flower-like fragrance. A really great Hock will have such a powerful bouquet that it can fill the room with its perfume soon after the cork is drawn.

Both in the bouquet and flavour of a white wine you will be on the look-out for any taint of sulphur. This may have been added to stop fermentation and leave some latent sugar in the wine, thus making it a sweet wine. Or the sulphur may have been added soon before bottling to cleanse and sterilize it, and so give it a longer life. Unfortunately, some wines have been given an overdose; you may occasionally detect it in a white Graves and the effect is unpleasant.

5. Choosing the Right Wine

All will agree that "only a fool mixes his drinks," but wherein lies his folly? Quite simply, the alcoholic products of barley and of the grape are enemies, and this is why he who takes whisky before (or after) wine is inviting a headache. Beer may go with gin; I am no judge of that, but certainly neither will go with wine. One small dry Martini before a meal may do little harm, though I do not recommend it, but several cocktails, heavy with gin, would be a foolish preliminary—and in any case would paralyse the taste for a wine of any delicacy. (It is almost—if not quite—as bad as tobacco. Sherry is the only wine that will stand up to tobacco-smoke, but the fact that one is drinking Sherry immediately before a meal is no excuse for the cigarette.) If you are physically low and feel you need the fillip of spirits before your dinner-guests arrive, let your pick-me-up be a dash of Three-star Brandy with soda or tonic water.

To drink a dry wine before a sweet one will always be the natural order. A fresh white Burgundy may be as delicious at the beginning of a meal as it would be out of place, after a red wine, at the end of it; indeed, all dry white wines are better before a red wine, just as a sweet white wine is better after the red.

As for Champagne, M. André Simon points out that you may suitably drink Champagne at almost any time or season. You may drink it right through a meal, as you may drink any other white wine, but the drier the wine the less pleasant will it be with the sweet course. And I think you will agree with Saintsbury when he said that he found the last glass of a white wine less attractive than the first, whereas the reverse was true about a red wine: for the red wine continually cleanses the palate as you drink it, and the sweeter white wines in particular most certainly do not. A *vin rosé*, from which one does not expect the highest qualities of either red or white wines, has one happy quality of its own—that of going pleasantly with almost any food with which wine can be drunk.

I admit it is not always easy to decide on the sequence of red wines at a meal. It would obviously be foolish to offer the best wines first and then tail away to the less good—and it may not be a simple matter to decide beforehand which *is* the better wine. Usually it is safe to serve the younger wines first; but what if the older has become rather feeble? It will seem even more frail than it is when drunk immediately after you have enjoyed a younger wine which happens to be full of vigour. But some men with great knowledge will invariably serve the younger wine first, while others will place their wines according to quality alone. Colonel Ian Campbell's views, in his chapter on Claret, should be carefully studied.

6. *Wines with Food*

The august President of the Wine and Food Society will, I am sure, agree with me when I say that the partnering of wines with food has raised enough problems to keep gastronomes arguing until Doomsday. Let me begin with a hardy perennial. Dare one drink red wine with fish?

A shocking thing, some say.

"Heavens, why ever not?" demands Mr. Frederick Cockburn. "They go perfectly well; I drink Claret often with fish."

Try the experiment yourself, if you will. I have done so, and I liked it not.

Gastronomically, to permit vinegar near wine is to desecrate the wine—it will turn it into vinegar. Let a squeeze of lemon in the salad-dressing give the necessary touch of tartness to the oil. Be more careful still with hors-d'oeuvre before a delicate wine.

Eggs, too, ought to be treated carefully if one is drinking a wine: the yolk tends to clog the taste a little and leave a tang of sulphur, neither of which will help one to appreciate a delicate red wine. Nothing can possibly stand up to a dish (however good it may be in itself) in which there is the heavy pungency of onion or the hot spice of curry. High seasoning, stinging the palate, dulls it to the caress of wine. With shellfish, also, one must go warily. Chablis is almost the traditional thing for an oyster. But whatever be your choice—and it is wide—do not drink any kind of spirits with shell-fish: in such close proximity these two will disagree.

CHEESE. With cheese we are again on debatable land. I have heard it maintained, and I am sure you have, that *any* wine will go with *any* cheese. While a mild or middling-mild cheese is a good cleanser of the palate, we must never forget that cheese is a savoury, and it seems to me to call for a touch of dryness in a white wine, while it combines admirably with Claret or red Burgundy. For a very delicate red wine I personally find that cheese like Gorgonzola is much too potent and leaves its own flavour too long on the palate. With the coarser cheeses the appropriate wine is, I think, a vigorous one of ordinary quality: certainly not a fine wine.

SWEETS. I am aware of no sweet, pudding, trifle or tart,

with which natural red wine will go well. If we must have wine with the sweet, the obvious thing is a sweet white wine. Sweets most assuredly to the sweet! Does any fruit go well with a red wine? Tawny Port is enjoyed by some with a really ripe pear and one or two other sweet fruits. A medlar that has reached the perfect stage of softness, and is just about to enter the stage of noble decay, goes excellently with Claret or Burgundy or indeed any natural red wine.

SUNDRY MEATS. In deciding on the wine to accompany the flesh of animal or bird, it is good to follow the rough plan I have suggested for cheeses: the more delicate wines for the more delicate flesh. I refer of course to red wines. Although most people would not object to a still white wine, if it were not too sweet, or to Champagne, I think that nothing can excel Claret. With roast beef, with the more strongly flavoured game, with venison, your choice had perhaps better be Burgundy.

NUTS AND WINE. With a glass of Port I can think of no better accompaniment than walnuts—although some of the big Kentish cobs and filberts run them pretty close. But nearly all nuts are good with Port—or indeed any red wine.

WINE IN THE KITCHEN. I would suggest that a little wine used in the cooking of certain dishes may add immensely to their attraction. The Empire wines, in particular, with their fairly pronounced flavour, can be a great help in the kitchen, and their reasonable price is an advantage.

Do not, I implore, listen to anyone who tells you that the lees of a wine after decanting—those unpleasant-looking lees heavy with deposit—should be used in cookery. The kitchen sink is the place for them.

7. Why should Wine Breathe?

Wine is said to "breathe" as it stands unstoppered or uncorked. Strictly speaking, it breathed from the very beginning of its life in cask, and also breathed the bubble of air left in the bottle on being corked. But the word is generally used

WINES AND FOOD

APÉRITIFS. One has a wide choice of wines that are fairly dry and so give an edge to the appetite: Sherry, Marsala, Madeira (Sercial), Champagne, a light German or Alsatian wine, a dry light Empire wine, Vermouth, etc. With them may be served olives, mild cheese-straws, etc.

DRY WHITE WINES. With Hors-d'oeuvre, Shell-fish, Fish, a dry type of any of the following:
> A white wine of Burgundy, the Rhône, the Rhine, the Moselle, Alsace, Italy, or British Empire.

RED WINES. With Entrée dishes, Liver, Kidneys, etc., Mutton, Beef, etc., Game, with or without Salad:
> Claret, Burgundy, a Rhône wine, an Italian or a natural Empire wine.

Many white wines, if not too dry, or a vin rosé, may be served instead of a red wine; Champagne is excellent with all white flesh; but Burgundy or Claret is the perfect accompaniment to most meats.

SWEET WHITE WINES. With Sweets and Dessert, one of the sweeter white wines:
> Sauternes, Barsac, a rich Graves, a sweet wine of Anjou, Italy or the British Empire, a full rich Hock or one of the less dry Champagnes.

With Cheese, either after or instead of a Sweet, a good red wine will generally be the most appropriate.

DESSERT WINES. With Port, Madeira, golden or brown Sherry, there are few better accompaniments than nuts.

If an old tradition be followed of serving a fine Claret or Burgundy at the end of the meal instead of a Dessert wine, note that a sweet white wine will not be a good preparation.

BRANDY, ETC. Cognac, Armagnac or liqueurs may be served with black coffee.

only when the wine is left open to the air before or after decanting.

Why should a red wine be allowed to breathe after it is uncorked? Quite simply, the contact with new air sets up a gentle activity in a healthy, living wine: it begins to express its character, to release its bouquet, to become more alive.

And even a rough young wine begins to soften and tries its best to please!

Some say that no wine should be given longer than six hours to breathe. I feel it dangerous to dogmatize. Many an *ordinaire* which I have drunk with quiet pleasure was more pleasing after twelve hours' breathing than after six. On the other hand, some wines will stand very little contact with the air before they become but a shadow of what they once were, and a wine of great delicacy or an old wine must be treated with care.

With more recent vintages—say those of the last twenty years or so—it is not likely that a wine will deteriorate in the span of a few hours: quite the reverse. A young or robust wine should, in short, breathe longer than a light, delicate, or old one.

It may be asked: Should I allow a white wine to breathe? White wine gives of its best soon after the cork is drawn. Obviously, a Champagne should be poured out at once. Uncork a Château d'Yquem, the *crème de la crème* of the Sauternes vineyards, and note how its powerful fragrance impregnates the air around. Fifteen minutes of breathing will suffice for such a wine—or for one of the important German wines or white Burgundies.

The more one learns of wine the more one finds that to make a rule is to invite an exception. As I said earlier, some white wines sold in Britain have a noticeable touch of sulphur in their bouquet and flavour. Very often the process of breathing, if accelerated, will get rid of much of it. By acceleration I mean the process of rapidly pouring the wine from one jug to another for a couple of minutes or so, in order to bring it vigorously into contact with the air. The wine can then be replaced in the bottle and put in the refrigerator. But this is a very different process from the gentle breathing which a fine red wine usually requires to bring it to its zenith.

8. The Question of Temperature

Any red wine can be best appreciated when it is at the temperature of a comfortably warm room. It will probably need several hours to reach this from a cellar temperature. Some experts say that a fine Claret is at its best at a slightly higher temperature than a good Burgundy, but this is a matter of opinion. There is pleasure to be had from noting how a wine expands and begins to give of its best as its temperature gently rises from the warmth of one's hand on the glass. The important thing is that the temperature of the wine must not be raised suddenly. But the red wines of Beaujolais, which are usually served while very young, are best drunk at cellar temperature.

In cooling white wines it is important to note that the sweeter the wine the colder it can be drunk. You can afford to chill a sweet white Bordeaux a good deal more than a dry wine of Montrachet or Meursault or one of the finer German wines. And do not serve Champagne too cold for its quality to be appreciated.

Indeed, no good white wine should be reduced much lower than 45 deg. F., for it becomes paralysed and the bouquet impaired. May I, in a horrified whisper, utter this warning: never, never, put ice *in* a fine white wine, still or sparkling.

Let me add that Port, rich dessert Sherry and Madeira are wines that should be drunk at the temperature of the room, whereas a pale or medium Sherry to be drunk early in a meal, or before it, should be at cellar coolness, or even a trifle lower.

9. The Art of Decanting

It is the deposit or the crust in the red wines that makes decanting necessary. With any everyday wine, like a young

Bordeaux or a fresh Beaujolais, you can please yourself. If there is no deposit, there is no need to decant: but by all means do so if you feel that the charm of a table is enhanced by a decanter of red wine, and I think most folk will agree that it is.

A white wine need not be decanted—I almost said *should* not—because it throws very little deposit. At the most, there may be a little pale, fine dust in the bottle.

There are two methods of decanting wine:

You may lift the bottle from the prone position in which it has been stored and slowly set it upright so that the crust will not be broken or the deposit will not be roughly thrown into the wine. If the wine is old, it should stand for at least twenty-four hours before you decant it. Better judges than I say that twelve are enough. A fine old wine is one of the few things on earth in which I would play for safety!

The other method is to lift the bottle carefully from the bin and prop it at such an angle that the wine will not spill when the cork is removed. In raising the bottle to this angle, be sure that you keep on top the side thât was uppermost in the bin. (With a crusted Port, your guide will be the white splash on the side of the bottle.) The only good use I know for a basket-cradle is to hold a bottle steady while you draw the cork. To serve wine with a heavy deposit straight from a bottle placed in one of these cradles means that the last few glasses are clouded because of the flowing back and forward of the wine as it is poured.

The wax or lead-foil capsule must be removed and the end of the cork cleaned of mould. The neck of the bottle must be wiped clean so that it is transparent. The corkscrew should penetrate the full length of the cork. After drawing, wipe the *inside* of the bottle-neck to remove any particles. And take care not to shake the bottle.

Have ready a candle that is burning with a good flame. An electric torch will do if its light does not dazzle the eye. While slowly pouring the wine into the decanter, see that the shoulder of the bottle is held above the light so that you can watch the slow shallow stream of wine as it flows through the neck. At the first sign of particles of deposit or crust passing along the neck, stop pouring. Unless you have a very steady hand, use a funnel.

10. *Approving and Serving*

Having decanted the wine, examine it to make certain that all is well. See that the bouquet is wholesome, although you cannot expect it to be already at its best. If you decide that something is wrong, you may have been warned of this by the state of the cork. The cork should be quite firm, with no signs of crumbling unless the wine is very old, and have a wholesome smell. If the wine is in the condition known as "corked," you will almost certainly detect this in the bouquet before you taste the wine; but tasting will give you final confirmation. A bad cork has a musty sourness that is most unpleasant.

Maybe the cork has stood vigorously up to its work, yet there is a smell of decay in the wine. This is perhaps caused by the disease of mildew, which often comes from too much rain at the wrong time of the year when the wine was vintaged. The beginner may find the *taste* of mildew more difficult to detect than the *smell* of it. To drink a badly mildewed wine is to be mournfully reminded of the onset of decay.

In tasting the wine you have decanted, make sure that it does not seem prematurely old. In a year when the general quality was good but the wines rather light, age is apt to come quickly. If on yet another day you should open a bottle that again shows signs of age it will be a warning to drink up your stock of this particular wine. One of the deepest regrets of a wine-lover is to recall how he hoarded half a dozen bottles of some admired vintage, only to find that under his very eyes they became aged.

"Bottle-sickness" is a fault you may not often come across. It happens to a young wine which finds itself locked up within the unfriendly prison of a bottle after being in a wooden cask where it had a good deal more air and freedom. The symptom of bottle-sickness is a harshness and "tanginess," which is a pretty plain hint that the wine has decided to sulk and go out of condition. A genuine bottle-sickness will usually pass off within a fairly short time.

If you are satisfied with the wine you have decanted, take it to a warm room so that it can breathe in peace and the temperature can rise slowly.

At table, you may wish to pour a little wine into your own glass first in case a guest's glass should receive an unexpected fragment of cork—and this you will be careful to remove with silver, not steel. Need I say that, with white wine as with red, no glass should be filled more than two-thirds? This allows the bouquet to be concentrated in the upper part of the glass.

One small item: Be sure never to wash your hands with a soap of a noticeable smell when you are going to handle or drink wine. Some soap-smells are apt to linger on the skin and can detract from the wine's bouquet. The late Francis Berry, a connoisseur with an extraordinarily fine palate, was known on occasion to send the server from the room with orders to "neutralize" his or her hands.

11. *In a Restaurant*

It is a difficult thing to choose a wine from a restaurant list with which you have had no previous experience. Far too often the descriptions of the wines are inadequate, and one gazes at names like Margaux, Graves, Beaune, Liebfraumilch in something very like despair.

The vintage year, the body of the wine, sweetness or dryness, and so forth, are the kind of facts one should be able to learn from a wine list—and which one should at least attempt to elicit from the waiter. Perhaps the best he can say is: "This one is very popular, sir; we've had no complaints." You are then faced with the alternative of closing your eyes and vaguely stabbing at the wine-list with the prong of a fork—or of ordering some beverage other than wine!

In a restaurant one must be on the look-out for the waiter who has received instructions to get rid of some particular wine—maybe a château-bottled Claret—because it is rapidly going downhill. I have had this experience in one of the best-known restaurants in the world, and the wine carried a famous name and was of an excellent vintage. Let it be noted that the wine was not "corked," it had no fault so glaring that one could reject it out of hand: it simply was ageing and not as good as it ought to have been, and certainly not worth the price asked.

One must guard against a notorious piece of restaurant barbarity—that of plunging a bottle of red wine into hot water. Marcel Boulestin, an exceptional *restaurateur*, ordered all his waiters never to do this even if the customer laid his hand on the bottle when presented to him and exclaimed: "Much too cold—take the chill off!" Four out of five wine-waiters will themselves suggest this to the customer. With a rough wine it matters little, but the process throws a fine wine off its balance.

You may bring your own bottle of wine to many hotels and restaurants if you pay corkage. The managers of some hotels state in their brochure that they charge corkage at two-and-sixpence or more per bottle, but it is always wise to inquire about this first and make some definite arrangement. You have the trouble of decanting your wine and carrying it to the restaurant, but at least you can be certain you will have the pleasure of giving your guests something they will enjoy.

12. Keeping a Wine Book

I recommend you to keep a Wine Book—that is, a manuscript book in which you note the date and place of every interesting wine you drink.

Against each bottle you should note details of bouquet, taste, farewell, and any other point of interest. If you think

the wine has not yet reached its best, jot this down: in half
a dozen years you may be able to test the accuracy of your
estimate. Some take pleasure in recording the foods that
accompanied the wines, and some note the names of hosts and
guests on each occasion.

With the example of Professor Saintsbury in front of you,
you could also keep in this book a Cellar section. Here you can
record each purchase, the name of the wine merchant, the
date and price, as well as the date on which you opened each
bottle.

Wine is a thing of delight. If we drink it as it deserves to be
drunk, with mind and body at ease and with our senses alert,
it yields a multiplicity of pleasures. And these are open to
most people to enjoy, for can a bottle of sound wine not be
bought for less than the cost of fifty cigarettes?

THE CONTRIBUTORS

To the writers who have contributed to this book I must express
my thanks.

M. André L. Simon, who has written the chapter on Champagne,
is the founder and President of the Wine and Food Society and is
the author of a shelf of wine books which are the fruits of scholarly
research and personal experience in the more important vineyards of
the world. Of Mr. H. Warner Allen, the well-known author, who
has contributed the chapter on Burgundy, it can be said that wine
has been his joy and recreation for over half a century. Mr. Charles
Williams, writer of the section on Sherry, a wine he has studied for
many years, is a familiar figure both in the City of London and in
the old town of Jerez; he was Chairman of the Wine Trade Club, and
I am grateful to him for many kind suggestions. The family of Mr.
Frederick Cockburn has for many generations been associated with
Port, and he has given us the benefit of knowledge and enthusiasm
which can almost be called hereditary. Among experts on Hock and
Moselle the name of Mr. Alfred Langenbach is well known; after a
long experience in the vineyards of the Rhine and the Moselle he has
published a book on them which is accepted as a work of the
highest authority. Mr. Stanley Davis, a popular lecturer on wine,
has put into a nutshell the essential facts about Alsatian wines, which
are becoming increasingly popular in Britain. From his early days

Mr. Frederick Rossi has known the winelands of Italy, and he gives us guidance on those wines which can be drunk both in their own country and in Britain. Mr. A. J. B. Rutherford, an acknowledged expert on Madeira, warns us that we must be careful in our choice of this wine, and his advice will help readers to a fuller enjoyment of it. Since mid-Victorian days, the name of Burgoyne has been linked with British Empire wines, and there could be no better guide than Mr. John Burgoyne, who clarifies difficulties and gives details of the great improvements in South African and Australian wines in recent years. In his chapter on Cognac the Hon. Frederick Hennessy has refrained from going too deeply into the intricacies of distillation and blending, but has marshalled the facts essential to one's enjoyment of what he calls "the heart of wine."

I have not yet mentioned Colonel Ian M. Campbell, who has contributed the opening chapter on the red wines of Bordeaux. Born in 1870, he is now the Grand Old Man among the connoisseurs of wine in Britain, and has written two charming books based on his memories of the long list of wines he has enjoyed. He counts himself above all a "Claret man"; and in his chapter the reader will share his joy in the red wines of Bordeaux, both old and new. Without stint, Colonel Campbell has given me the benefit of his advice in the making of this book, and it now gives me pleasure to record my gratitude.

AUGUSTUS MUIR.

REVISED EDITION—EDITOR'S NOTE

The death of Colonel Campbell sadly deprived us of his expert judgment on recent vintages, particularly on those of the wine he most enjoyed, claret; and I have added notes to the Bordeaux chapter and others to bring them up to date.

I should like to acknowledge with gratitude the help given to me, in this latest revision of the text, by my friend Kenneth Christie, Master of Wine. It is my hope that this book will continue to be helpful to all who, by acquiring more knowledge and a keener sense of discrimination, wish to enhance their pleasure in wine.

A.M.

I · THE RED WINES OF BORDEAUX

BY IAN M. CAMPBELL

CLARET holds an exalted place among wines. It is a perfectly natural wine, the product of the complete, natural fermentation of the juice of red grapes. Whether it should be called the queen of wines, as it is by some people, matters little: certainly, by reason of its gentleness and refinement of character and breeding, it would not be unworthy of the title.

Personally (and I have known it intimately for more than half a century), because of its being natural and simple, gracious and pleasing, I prefer to call it the mother of the family of wines. A well-informed familiarity with Claret will help us to know and appreciate all wines.

Although not perhaps the largest, Great Britain is the most genuinely appreciative consumer of Claret in the world, apart from Bordeaux itself, and until the advent of Whisky it was almost the national drink of Scotland. Claret has been a bond between Bordeaux and Britain since the days of the Plan-

24

tagenets, when the Province of Gascony, or part of it, came
by marriage under the English Crown. King Richard II of
England was born in Bordeaux, and the wines of Gascony
were shipped from there to London for hundreds of years
under the auspices of the Vintners' Company, who dealt
drastically with any rogues or impostors by confiscating and
pouring into the river their false or adulterated wines—and
sometimes forcing the miscreants to swallow their own
unsavoury counterfeit concoctions!

Today the bond is still strong, and many of the Bordeaux
folk are English-speaking. They make admirable hosts and
lay themselves out to welcome the stranger within their gates.
My own experience over many years is that a visitor from
Britain is sure of a warm and homely welcome. One of the four
big cities of France, Bordeaux has a magnificent Renaissance
opera-house that adds beauty and dignity to its main square,
while other squares and open spaces are devoted to well-
planted gardens· of semi-tropical appearance enclosed by
houses of somewhat old-fashioned but stately architecture.
The county, or *département,* of which Bordeaux is the capital
is called Gironde, but it is the River Garonne whose banks
are adorned by the handsome quays and buildings of this
busy, prosperous, wine-perfumed port; and not until a few
miles north of Bordeaux is the Garonne joined by the Dordogne, to flow in happy mud-coloured confluence northwards
to the Bay of Biscay under the name Gironde.

As you sail upstream towards the city you cannot but be
struck by the vast expanse of vineyards that cover the flat-
looking country on your right hand. That is the famous Médoc
—the very name of which stirs expectations. On the opposite
bank, and on many of the green islets in the brown waters of
the estuary, you will see flourishing vineyards. Even the
cottage gardens along the banks of the Gironde, Garonne and
Dordogne are not too small for a patch of vine, from which a
precious *barrique* or two of wine may be garnered.

The stranger who visits the vineyards for the first time may well express surprise at the stony and impoverished appearance of the soil, but the roots of the vine are wise and dig deep to forage for their nourishment. Indeed, the soil receives as careful and skilful treatment from the owner of the vineyard as do the vines themselves. The native soil of a wine plays an important part in its character, quality and evolution.

Different exposure to sunshine and rain, to heat and cold, and various slopes of the ground, will affect the development of the fruit and consequently of the wine made from it. Discovery of the best species of vine, *Vitis vinifera,* to be planted in the particular soils must have given many a headache to viticulturists in the past and called for many years, perhaps centuries, of trial and error. In the Bordeaux vineyards the Cabernet-Sauvignon grape is the most dependable and distinguished and, in consequence, the most widely planted. And experiments have conclusively proved that the vines of the Gironde may be planted in similar soil in vineyards anywhere else in the world but will not produce a vine resembling Claret, except perhaps in colour.

The Vintage in the Gironde takes place in late summer or early autumn. It is the great festival of the year. Like the harvesters and hop-pickers of Britain, the *vendange rs* are almost a fraternity apart, with their own codes and traditions: this is their Season, a short one but strenuous, gay and good-humoured. The weather has been anxiously watched all through the spring and summer by every vineyard proprietor. People in Britain know how a fruit crop can be ruined by one disastrous night of frost. Even in Bordeaux, which is four hundred and fifty miles nearer the equator than London, a late frost may play havoc in the vineyards. There are other dangers—phylloxera, mildew, black-rot, oidium, etc.—against which constant watch has to be kept and remedies speedily supplied. I fear that we pay scant heed to the troubles and worries of the *vignerons* who provide us with our glass of fine wine!

In vivid contrast to the habitually peaceful atmosphere

that pervades the *chais* (wine-storehouses) and cellars of the vineyard, during the Vintage season the most lively animation and excitement can be seen among the vines and in the press-houses—an animation that is on a par with the liquid turmoil fussing and foaming in the giant casks and vats where the grape juice, now called the "must," fermenting with hot, bubbling enthusiasm, is converting all its sugar into alcohol and carbon dioxide to become wine: a natural and wonderful metamorphosis.

The ripe grapes, having been carefully picked from the vines, are at once heaped up in the *cuviers*—square, open troughs. The juice is squeezed out, sometimes by men dancing and stamping on them and sometimes by hand or mechanical press, and quickly transferred to the big vats where the germs of fermentation will carry on their boisterous operations. Fermentation may last for a fortnight or more before the test-ing instrument shows that the "must" has converted all its sugar. The young wine is now drawn off the vats into hogs-heads, which lie in rows in the overground cellars. All useless and harmful sediments, pips, skins, bits of stalk, and so on, will sink to the bottom; then the clear wine is carefully drawn off the lees into empty barrels. This process, called "racking," may be repeated two or three times. Generally some two and a half years will have passed before a good wine is considered to be fit for bottling or for export in the cask.

When once the wine is safely in bottle, all it asks for is to be left alone quietly lying in its box or its bin in a cool cellar with a more or less permanent temperature of about 54 deg. Fahrenheit until it has matured sufficiently for pleasurable consumption. This may be in a year's time, if the Claret is a cheap wine for daily drinking, or in five, ten or twenty years according to the quality of the wine and the characteristics of the year of its birth.

For immediate drinking, few wine merchants in Britain will ever send out Claret of even very moderate quality until it has been in bottle, or "under the cork" as they may possibly term it, for at least twelve months. The humbler, lower-quality wines will then have lost something of the rough greenness of youth. I confess I have drunk and enjoyed Claret which has been less than a year in bottle, but I have taken it more as a thirst-quencher than as an *objet d'art*. I allude to it, however, because I wish to go to the other extreme and refer to the achievable longevity of Claret by mentioning that I have also lingered contentedly over a high-grade Claret, a Château Larose, when it was a hundred years old, that is to say about ninety-eight years in bottle, and found it sweet, soft, genteel, wonderfully well preserved, very interesting to savour and enjoyable to drink. But few are the Clarets that will live for a hundred years!

It may have struck the reader that I have described the old Larose as being "sweet," after having stated in an earlier paragraph that in the course of fermentation all the sugar of the grape juice or "must" has been transformed. It is a provision of Nature that after complete fermentation there will still remain in most vintages, more pronounced in some than in others, *a perceptible element of sweetness* in the new wines, for which we may be thankful and which may be more in evidence as the wine matures. I always turn aside from a Claret, or a Claret vintage, that seems to me hard and lacking in that delicate sweetness which in my opinion is one of its necessary attributes and charms.

The richly endowed Gironde is itself divided into several regions. The three best known are the Médoc, Graves and St. Émilion. These are the homes of Claret, though the Graves district produces a large quantity of white wine as well, and the Médoc a small quantity. These districts show distinctive characteristics in the style and flavour of their Clarets, and some good judges will tell you at once from which of them the Claret you give them comes. There are a few who will be competent to go further and tell you, and that correctly, the château or vineyard of the wine and the year of its vintage. But such skill, though much to be admired—and envied—is not essential to a real and unaffected enjoyment of Claret. The ability thus displayed, however, is one of the rewards that come to the enthusiastic student of Claret and indicates a trained nose, a critical palate and a good memory, things which any real wine-lover can in some measure acquire.

In the southern part of the Médoc—the Haut Médoc—are produced the finest wines in the world. St. Émilion has a satellite, a very independent one, called Pomerol, which produces some very pleasing and popular wines. Although in Great Britain people often talk of "Graves" as a white wine, with which the name has come to be identified, there is actually more red wine than white produced in this picturesque area—and superlatively fine Clarets indeed some of them are. It was the red wines of Graves that first established the good name and renown of Claret.

In addition to these three favoured regions, several others produce good wines of a quality less outstanding than those of the big three, the three Graces. Between the converging courses of the Rivers Garonne and Dordogne there lies a triangle-shaped district of broken country replete with vineyards and known as Entre-deux-Mers; and Côtes or uplands rising from the rivers extend along the north shores of the Garonne and the Gironde; while the low-lying sandy banks of the rivers are designated Palus, meaning marshland.

Many who are eager to know how to choose and enjoy Claret hesitate through fear of displaying ignorance (a weakness we all share) to take the necessary first steps. I wonder how many friends have said to me: "I wish I knew more about Claret." Few of us are born with a taste for Claret any more than for poetry, mathematical science or Gorgonzola cheese; it is acquired. I always mention this in order to prevent the irresolute student from being put off by a possible failure to find his first glass of Claret exactly as big and sugary and warming as he may have expected it to be. There is by nature a delicacy, a cool refinement, amounting almost to a shyness, about Claret that will be recognized but perhaps not understood when first its acquaintance is made, but which soon prove to be part of its irresistible charm.

What *is* the best way, then, to know how to select and enjoy Claret? In practically every city and town in the United Kingdom you will find a wine merchant; he is the best line of approach at the outset. He is there to please and teach; he lives by his knowledge and experience; and, if he is a really good one, he will be only too ready to pass on the benefit of these to his clients. But the best instructors of all will be the bottles of Claret you share with those friends who, like yourself, are intelligently and aesthetically anxious to fathom the measureless delights of the study and "companionship" of Claret.

The wine in the bottle is a living entity, in a state of growth up to an indefinite age, and thereafter in a state of decline perhaps very slow. It is shocked by extremes of heat and cold. It requires a rest after a journey and to be treated always with care and respect. There is also a certain ritual you can observe, at your own or a wine-loving friend's table or in a restaurant, but which will be taboo at a dinner party. First, the connoisseur raises his glass up to the light; he does this to see that the wine is clear and bright and of a good colour. You will notice that he then seems thoughtfully to smell the wine: this he does to satisfy himself that its *bouquet* is clean and free from any taint of cork or anything else that is foreign to good Claret. These moments of alert, critical interest are of immense value to the expert. Then and only then will he take a small sip of the wine, followed maybe by a second one as if to confirm his first impression.

I have no use for the fellow I so often see in the restaurant who, when the waiter very correctly pours a thimbleful of wine, for approval, into his customer's glass, seizes the glass and, with the air of a Great Mogul, rapidly tosses the contents down his throat while he gives an approbatory nod to the gratified waiter. It is a mistake, often regretted, not to smell the wine first, as your nose is generally far more sensitive than your perhaps distracted palate when a hurried decision is required.

We now have the brief procedure invariably followed by the genuine and unostentatious expert: SEE, SMELL, SIP, and his guests can safely join him in the final act of SWALLOW. One critic of a little book I wrote about wine objected to the word "swallow" in this connexion, but I cannot imagine what else you can do with the wine in your glass if the three previous tests have satisfied you!

A noted work of high authority, *Bordeaux et ses Vins*, published in Bordeaux by Feret, gives particulars of some three thousand·five hundred *crus*, or vineyards, which annually produce red or white wine, or both. In 1855 a classification in five divisions was drawn up by the Bordeaux *courtiers* (wine brokers) of the more prominent wines of the Médoc at that date, based on their estimation and marketable values over a period of years. The list, which has held its own up to the present day, contained the names of sixty-one *crus*, known as the Classed Growths, of the Médoc and one chosen from the Graves district (Château Haut-Brion). It was a great honour to be among the classed growths; and although the number of the select few might today be increased by further additions from Médoc, Graves, St. Émilion, and possibly Pomerol, it would be very difficult to dethrone any one of those already chosen. A mistake to be avoided is the underrating of a wine because it is only a fourth- or fifth-classed growth; in some years, one or other of these can be among the best of the vintage.

MEDOC
Premiers Crus

Château	Commune
LAFITE	PAUILLAC
MARGAUX	MARGAUX
LATOUR	PAUILLAC
HAUT-BRION	PESSAC (GRAVES)

Deuxièmes Crus

Château	Commune
MOUTON-ROTHSCHILD	PAUILLAC
RAUSAN-SÉGLA	MARGAUX
RAUSAN-GASSIES	,,
LÉOVILLE-LAS-CASES	ST. JULIEN
LÉOVILLE-POYFERRÉ	,,
LÉOVILLE-BARTON	,,
DURFORT-VIVENS	MARGAUX
LASCOMBES	,,
GRUAUD-LAROSE	ST. JULIEN
BRANE-CANTENAC	CANTENAC
PICHON-LONGUEVILLE-BARON	PAUILLAC
PICHON-LONGUEVILLE-LALANDE	,,
DUCRU-BEAUCAILLOU	ST. JULIEN
COS-D'ESTOURNEL	ST. ESTÈPHE
MONTROSE	,,

Troisièmes Crus

KIRWAN	CANTENAC
ISSAN	,,
LAGRANGE	ST. JULIEN
LANGOA	,,
GISCOURS	LABARDE
MALESCOT-SAINT-EXUPÉRY	MARGAUX
CANTENAC-BROWN	CANTENAC
PALMER	,,
LA LAGUNE	LUDON
DESMIRAIL (production ceased)	MARGAUX
CALON-SÉGUR	ST. ESTÈPHE
FERRIÈRE	MARGAUX
MARQUIS D'ALESME-BECKER	,,
BOYD-CANTENAC	,,

Quatrièmes Crus

Château	Commune
ST. PIERRE (SEVAISTRE AND BONTEMPS)	ST. JULIEN
BRANAIRE-DUCRU	,,
TALBOT	,,
DUHART-MILON	PAUILLAC
POUGET	CANTENAC
LA TOUR-CARNET	ST. LAURENT
ROCHET	ST. ESTÈPHE
BEYCHEVELLE	ST. JULIEN
LE PRIEURÉ	CANTENAC
MARQUIS DE TERME	MARGAUX

Cinquièmes Crus

PONTET-CANET	PAUILLAC
BATAILLEY	,,
HAUT-BATAILLEY	,,
GRAND-PUY-LACOSTE	,,
GRAND-PUY-DUCASSE	,,
LYNCH-BAGES	,,
LYNCH-MOUSSAS	,,
DAUZAC	LABARDE
MOUTON-D'ARMAILHACQ	PAUILLAC
LE TERTRE	ARSAC
HAUT-BAGES-LIBÉRAL	PAUILLAC
PÉDESCLAUX	,,
BELGRAVE	ST. LAURENT
CAMENSAC	,,
COS-LABORY	ST. ESTÈPHE
CLERC-MILON	PAUILLAC
CROIZET-BAGES	,,
CANTEMERLE	MACAU

HCW—B

A large number of the vineyards of Bordeaux call them-selves *"Château"* even if the *soi-disant* castle be only a cottage: it is a recognized and quite convenient custom. It will be noticed that opposite each of the *châteaux* is given the name of the *commune* (township) within whose area the *château* and its vineyard lie. The *commune* of Pauillac con-tains the largest number of classed growths, being followed by St. Julien, then Margaux and Cantenac (often bracketed together) and St. Estèphe. At the head of the second class is the famous Château Mouton-Rothschild, which so many connoisseurs consider should be in the first class. Château Margaux is in the *commune* of Margaux, and the student must learn to differentiate between the noble *château* and a *vin ordinaire* from its neighbourhood. There are, I regret to say, a few dishonest restaurants where they will try to pass off "Margaux" as *Château* Margaux. Do not be deceived; if you want Château Margaux, look at the bottle and see that you get the wine. If the wine has been bottled by its proprietors at the château itself it will have that fact, its name and vintage stated on the cork. See the cork. Château Margaux at its best can be unmatchable, a very noble wine.

With an almost political sagacity the proprietors, brokers and merchants have built up a social order wherein vineyards not in the list of classed growths are termed *Bourgeois Supérieurs*, those a trifle lower are *Bourgeois*, and below them again come *Artisans*. This gradation applies to the Médoc only; Graves and St. Émilion have each a structure of their own, based on the crucial tests of time and experience.

Some of the wines of what may be called the middle classes, *Bourgeois* and *Bourgeois Supérieurs*, are of excellent quality and good value for daily drinking, especially in these sorry days when most incomes are restricted by harassing taxation. Under normal conditions I would have recommended seekers after a satisfactory routine to make a good *Bourgeois* wine their daily portion and keep their classed growths for enter-tainment purposes and special occasions.

On the age at which Claret ought to be drunk I can lay down no precise or immutable rule. So much depends on the constitution, not only of a particular wine, but, even more, of a particular vintage; and there are exceptions to every theory that may be advanced. Most Clarets of the sturdy 1870 vintage were hardly ready to drink when fifty years old, while nearly all the sweet ripe wines of 1875 were practically dead and buried long before they could arrive at such an age.

These two wines of the 'seventies remind me how greatly my education was enriched by a close companionship with the wines of that remarkable decade. The wine of 1871, disregarded in its early days, proved to be "a gem of purest ray serene," light, fragile, with an aroma of flowers and a taste of ripe fruit. Many have said it was the consummation of Claret. Today, 1872 and 1873 would have received good marks, but they were lost in the crowd of beauty that surrounded them. 1874s were great wines, with charm and perfect balance: they were the avowed rivals of 1875s, probably the most popular Claret of the magnificent decade of the 'seventies. The '75s were light but abounding in sunshine and sugar and delicious flavours. I found them entrancing, and, thanks to my residence in Bordeaux in 1892 and 1893, I did justice to them in their prime. Although at the outset praised by some of the know-alls, the wines of 1876 were soon neglected, and unfortunately a slight acidity showed itself in the 1877s as the wine left the palate, and minimized their undoubted charm. Phylloxera, that ruthless enemy of the vine, was already mustering its forces for a mass attack; but 1878, full of sunshine, made its appearance in time to give us a good, full, sweet wine, not so refined as its predecessors of '77 and '75, but well-balanced and fruity. The vintage has done a great work for Claret in linking up the pre-phylloxera wines with those that were produced by the replacing vines. I heard Hilaire Belloc say that an *impériale* of 1878 Latour was the finest Claret he had ever drunk. It might be said that vintage 1879 let the team down and disgraced the famous decade, but it was the victim

of circumstances and the inroads of the loathsome subter-
ranean pest of phylloxera. Even so, one or two classed growths
of the year won through and were drinkable. Yet, however
loudly I acclaim the 'seventies as a wonderful decade, none of
its wines in my opinion was equal to the 1864 Lafite—the
finest Claret I ever drank: a splendid memory.

I shall pass quickly over the 'eighties and 'nineties. Some
good, indeed some excellent, wines were made in those
decades, although many were rather hard and dry, and some
of the wines of the 'eighties had a mere mawkish sweetness.
The wines of 1893 were fine and big and supple, but a touch
of acidity has kept them from being reckoned quite first-rate.
I have a different story to tell of 1899 and 1900, the Darby
and Joan of post-phylloxera Claret. These two are now grace-
fully and sweetly passing away, and perhaps not many of the
new Claret lovers of today will catch a glimpse of them—and
those will be specially privileged who have this pleasure. They
will, however, enjoy a heritage denied to us old folk. They will
see the promising wines of the 'forties in full stature, when
ripe and ready, and I feel sure they will sing their praises as
loudly and as faithfully as we have sung those of bygone
favourites. But before I talk of the 'forties I shall offer brief
notes on the intervening decades.

Although many good, interesting and attractive wines were
made in the years that followed the magnificent vintage of
1900, neither of the first two decades of this century can be
called great. The giant-like Haut-Brion of 1906 is still very
much alive; so is the Cheval Blanc and the Brane-Cantenac.
But neither decade is nearly as important as the 'twenties. I
fear we can only envy those who still have a few bottles left of
1920, 1923 and 1924—and even 1926 and 1928 and 1929 are
becoming very scarce. He is lucky who is given a chance of
tasting some of the best of these vintages, particularly of 1929,
whose sweet fruity wines are delicious and much riper than
those of either 1926 or 1928. The year 1929 was a splendid
vintage year! The 1928 wines are developing very slowly,

but are fine, big, generous fellows. A chance of tasting 1924 Lafite, Latour or Mouton-Rothschild should not be missed, nor one of making the acquaintance of the 1923 Haut-Brion, the astonishing 1921 Cheval Blanc, the 1920 Latour.

Clarets of the 1934 vintage were very good, and the greater wines should give pleasure for some years to come. But the wines of 1937 have puzzled those who phophesied a great future for them. They have been developing terribly slowly, and I fear many of them may be old before they are completely ripe: still, it was a well-constituted vintage and some of its classified growths will, I hope, turn up trumps eventually. It was a real misfortune that there were not more vintages of even average merit in the 'thirties.

It says a great deal for the esteem in which the 1943 vintage was held that very soon its wines were difficult to find. If war conditions prevented them from being really outstanding, they were good, well-balanced, fairly sweet, medium-bodied wines.

The wines of the 1944 vintage were on the light side, but were refined and well-knit. Although they had no very pronounced bouquet, what appealed to me especially was the delightful sweetness that characterised them ever since I first tasted them in 1945. Coming between the decidedly more robust 1943s and the even more *puissant* 1945s, they were, in my opinion, rather mistakenly neglected both in Britain and Bordeaux.

The wines of 1945 put all previous war vintages in the shade. They captured the imagination and the market as rich, generous, full-bodied wines, which would obviously take some years to arrive at their best, owing perhaps to a natural overweight of tannin.

The 1946 vintage was of a different style and calibre altogether: its wines were healthy and well-made but appeared to me to be skinny and hard, and short of sugar after the far fruitier 1945s. It reminds me too much of a vintage exactly fifty years its predecessor, the 1896, which only required a

little more sweetness and a little less of a chilly stand-offishness
to have ensured it the highest honours. Too much sugar, on
the other hand, can so upset a wine's balance as to be even
more disastrous. We had a striking example of that in the
vintage of 1921, when the excess of sugar caused a secondary
fermentation and ruined most of the wine of the year. The
Cheval Blanc was of course a brilliant exception, and I have
heard people appraise it as being the most remarkable claret
they have ever tasted.

The 1947 wines were fairly full-bodied, well-balanced with
delightful flavour and bouquet, great distinction in the higher
growths, and sufficient sweetness. I prefer them to the 1945s.

The year 1948 had many admirers too; and the 1949s have
greatly added to the prestige of the "fascinating 'forties".

More than once I have mentioned the word "well-
balanced." To be a genuine, lasting success a wine must
possess a perfect balance. I hope I may be excused if I quote
some words on this point which I wrote a few years ago: "In
all wines a *perfect* balance may mean the approach to the
unattainable will-o'-the-wisp perfection, but a *good* balance is
absolutely essential: and by 'balance' is meant, untechnically
speaking, the relatively correct proportion in the wine of all
vinous ingredients, mineral, vegetable, and chemical, such as
water, sugar, tannin, alcohol, ethers, and so on, requisite to
show health, strength, quality and promise of tip-top normal
development. Unless a wine has that good balance it may
charm for a while, but it will not endure: and the better the
breed of the wine, the more necessary the good balance."

Let me offer you a word of counsel of a more general kind.
It is safer to buy a wine with a less illustrious name but
of a fine vintage year than even a wine of the first growth of
a doubtful or inferior year. There will be exceptions, and a
chance may sometimes be worth taking, but not often. If a
wine is constitutionally unsound, diseased, mildewed or
tainted, as a wine of a really poor vintage year may be, it will
never be good, however long you may keep it.

The ideal temperature at which Claret should be drunk is that of the dining-room, but how is that to be attained? I deprecate all last-moment devices such as placing the decanter of wine in front of the fire, or even worse a scorching electric stove; or rinsing the decanter with hot water immediately before decanting, or plunging it into hot water after decanting; or by heating in one way or another the wineglasses. Such practices risk serious impairment of the wine. I cannot too often repeat that wine is a living organism, very sensitive to sudden changes of temperature which benumb its vitality, and Claret, owing to the delicacy of its nature, is more likely than other wines to suffer. The wine should be allowed to stand long enough in a comfortably warm atmosphere to reach the temperature of the air around it. Although I prefer Claret to be too cool rather than too warm, I must admit that it does not show at its best if served very cold, but the warmth of the hand put round the bowl of the wineglass, together with the temperature of the room itself, will soon convey to a cellar-cold wine a natural and acceptable warmth.

May I repeat what I said at the beginning? I consider a good knowledge and appreciation of Claret to be the most reliable background to an understanding and appreciation of all other wines. I can speak as a regular wine-drinker who has enjoyed, and still enjoys, I am grateful to say, all good wines whatever their colour and whencesoever they come. Let me quote the words of a wine-lover whom I knew well and could influence little, a very gifted Irishman of the name of Maurice Healy, barrister, soldier, orator, and author of a delightful book, *Stay Me With Flagons*: "Claret is wine. It is the wine. It is entirely natural. It is almost infinite in its variety. It is lovely in its colour, lovely in its fragrance, lovely in its flavour, lovely in its companionship. It is free alike from headiness and from heaviness; it is digestible itself and a good digestive as well." I endorse that eulogy.   I.M.C.

RECENT VINTAGES

In the nineteen-fifties, we have a number of interesting vintages, each with a character of its own.

The wines of 1950 were soft and medium-bodied. Although they were not rated in early years in the very top class, many of them have developed remarkably and are much better than some judges expected. But nobody would claim them to be as good as the wines of 1952, which excelled particularly in St. Emilion and Pomerol. (Often we find that in these two districts they were more successful than in the Médoc: and, just as often, the reverse is the case.)

The wines of 1953 were full-flavoured, fruity, and most of them have matured more quickly than the firmer 1952s.

Well-balanced wines were made in 1955; in St. Emilion and Pomerol many were above the average for these districts.

Due to the destructive frost early in 1956, which killed off many vines, the yield in 1957 was small. Most of the wines were rather severe and harsh, but they have been softening and, with any luck, may yet be very much better than they were. I am allowing a few bottles of 1957 claret to sleep peacefully in my cellar in the hope that one day they will surprise me—as some hard, unresponsive wines have done in the past. The most remarkable example was the wine of 1870, which was as stubborn as a mule and ended by captivating everyone by its charm.

The clarets of 1958 were never very highly thought of; but many of them are very pleasant little luncheon wines, light in body, delicate, maturing very quickly. Particularly in the Médoc and Graves, some fairly good wines were made.

In 1959, shouts of applause welcomed the round, full, fruity wine, which had so greatly benefited by the wonderful summer weather: but if the applause was just a trifle too loud, and if this wine could hardly be called the claret of the century, it is far above the average. One can go ranging among the bourgeois growths—which are too often ignored—and pick many a winner: the search is well worth while. It was a year that gave every vineyard in the Gironde a chance to produce the best claret it could make; and most of the wines of 1959 can be taken as characteristic of its own particular vineyard and well up to its best traditions. If I could not claim for these wines all the virtues of the great 1929s, nevertheless we should be grateful for this vintage of exactly thirty years later.

Rain fell in grim and funereal earnest in 1960. Too much rain and not enough sunshine will play the devil in a vineyard. Fortunately, the sun had shone in the early weeks of summer and gave the grapes a good start. There was a big crop, but the wines were lacking in tannin and came too quickly to maturity so that they were drinkable after an unusually short spell in bottle.

The chilling frost that descended in 1961 while the vines were in flower might have utterly ruined the vintage: in fact, it killed about half the crop and brought despair to every vigneron. But Mother Nature made reparation, as she often does, though not always so quickly as she did in 1961. Beautiful summer weather gave every chance to the grapes that survived the frost, and all the strength of the vines was concentrated on them. It turned out to be a remarkable vintage, small as it was: some maintain it was the best since 1929, better than 1959—and time will tell. It is not a wine to drink up quickly, particularly the better growths: rather it is one to keep, opening a bottle at intervals to note how it has matured. The St. Emilions and Pomerols excelled themselves in that wonderful year.

The fact that the wines of 1962 are not in the same class as those of 1961 can again be put down to weather, which retarded the flowering of the vines, and there was a lack of rain until September, when it came just too late to give a happy ending to the anxious story of that rather arid summer. The thirsty grapes swelled quickly under the September showers but had no time to develop the sugar and other constituents needed to make a great vintage. There was an enormous crop of smooth, pleasant wine with too little tannin and less alcohol than the wines of 1961 possessed. In the Médoc and Graves, the wines were noticeably fuller than those of St. Emilion and Pomerol.

On the whole, I am afraid that the clarets of 1963 were rather a poor lot. When vineyards refuse to sell their wine under their own château labels and get rid of a vintage for blending with ordinaires, you may be sure the wine-growers are unhappy about its quality. As usual, there were exceptions. Perhaps the most notable was the wine of Latour: but how often, in indifferent years, has Château Latour surprised us all with wine a good deal better than merely good!

Of the 1964s, many fine and also many indifferent wines were made and some thoroughly poor ones. In vineyards where the grapes were gathered before the rain came pelting down on 8th October, the wines turned out well. In the commune of St. Julien in the Médoc, there were quite a number that were fortunate; and in St. Emilion and Pomerol, some really good wines were made. It is a vintage in which careful choice is necessary.

Since 1964 there have been two wonderful vintages, 1966 and 1970. Among the other vintages, a buyer should go very carefully and take the best advice he can find before making a purchase.

How many of the wines on which I have been commenting will "make old bones"? We can but wonder. Since the Second World War, the clamant demand has been for wines that will rapidly mature and soon become silky on the palate. Removal of all the stalks, removal of skin and pips, a short fermentation period, frequent rackings and so forth—all this will produce the desired result: but the wines when they reach bottle, pleasant as they may become in a remarkably short time, can never slowly mature and reveal in due time, before they fade into senility, the complex splendours of the wines that were made by the *méthode ancienne*.   A.M.

RED GRAVES, ST. ÉMILION, POMEROL

The following are among the best known vineyards. Editor.

RED GRAVES: Haut-Brion (classed as a First Growth with the Médoc wines), Carbonnieux, Domaine de Chevalier, Ferran, Fieuzal, Haut-Bailly, Haut-Brion Larrivet, La Louvière, La Mission Haut-Brion, Olivier, Pape Clément, Pique-Caillou, Pontac-Monplaisir, Smith-Haut-Lafitte.

ST. ÉMILION: Cheval Blanc, Ausone, L'Angélus, Canon, Canon-La-Gaffelière, Beausejour, Cadet-Bon, Clos Fourtet, Coutet, Figeac Pavie, Pavie-Decesse, Domaine de Pavie-Macquin, Troplong-Mondot, Yon-Figeac.

POMEROL: Pétrus, Certan, La Conseillante, Clos l'Église, Domaine de l'Église, L'Évangile, Nénin, Petit-Village, Trotanoy, Vieux-Château-Certan.

❧ ❧ ❧

SOME CLARET VINTAGES SINCE 1949

1949 Very good; soft	1962 Good
1952 Very good; firm wines	1964 Many very good wines
1953 Very good; fruity, soft	1966 Excellent
1955 Very good wine	1967 Many good wines
1959 Very good; full	1969 Some very good wines
1960 Fair; light	1970 Excellent
1961 Excellent	1971 Mediocre; some good wines

THE WHITE WINES OF BORDEAUX

BY AUGUSTUS MUIR

IN addition to its red wines, the Gironde produces large quantities of white wine, grown in four main areas and a number of smaller ones.

In the largest of them, Entre-deux-Mers, a triangle of land between the Dordogne and Garonne rivers, most of the wines are sent to co-operative cellars to be blended, so that a fairly constant standard can be maintained. They are medium-sweet, of no great body, but are a useful type of "café" wine.

The white wines of the Graves district (where in fact more red wine than white is made) range from fairly dry to slightly sweet; but sweetness is a relative term, and the sweetest Graves is drier than Sauternes. Much of the cheaper Graves sold in Britain is poor stuff; it is wise to pay more and have a wine of some character. The named blend of a good shipper will not greatly vary, and familiar names include: Bel Enclos, Ch. Montbrun Goutte d'Or, Clos-des-Roches, Graves Dry Royal, Graves Monopole Dry, La Vigne Blanche, Maison d'Or, Rosechatel.

Opposite Graves, on the right bank of the Garonne, we find white wines known as Premières Côtes de Bordeaux. Langoiran and Cadillac are among the best known of the twenty-two parishes in this long narrow strip of land.

Moving up-river among the vineyards of some of the most charming hill-slopes in the Gironde we come to a little group of districts which produce wines of distinctly better quality. The first one we enter is Loupiac, with wines moderately high in alcohol and full flavoured, some of which have been described as worthy to rank as among the classed growths of Sauternes. The wines of Ste.-Croix-du-Mont, also well known in Britain, are fairly sweet, rich and full. The neighbouring area of St. Macaire also produces sweet wines of good body.

On the opposite side of the river is the region of Cérons.

The wines not only of the parish itself, but also those of Podensac and Illats, are permitted to use this controlled name. These have always been regarded as part of the great Graves district, and the name Graves may still be used on the labels. These wines have been described as a kind of halfway house between the generality of Graves wines and the greater wines of Sauternes. Highly perfumed and fairly full-bodied, most of them are suitable to drink with the sweets course of a meal if one wishes a wine of good quality but not so expensive or so richly sweet as a fine Sauternes.

The wines of Sauternes—or of "Sauternes and Barsac," to give the area is official name—are quite outstanding among the white wines of Bordeaux. Both Sauternes and Barsac are among the best-known white wines in the world, and there is a fairly distinct difference between them. The Barsac is less highly perfumed and less luscious than a Sauternes; it has a more nutty flavour and usually has just a hint of dryness in its after-taste; but nearly all of them are semi-sweet (unless, on occasion, a wine on the dry side is deliberately made) and some are very sweet. Château Coutet and Château Climens have the pride of place among over eighty vineyards in the parish of Barsac.

The Sauternes-and-Barsac area includes also the three parishes of Preignac (with Château de Suduiraut as its principal vineyard), Bommes, and Fargues. In 1855, when the red wines of the Médoc were classified, a classification was also made in this area, and the parish of Bommes had the honour of finding six of its vineyards marked up as First Growths, among them Château La Tour-Blanche and Château de Rayne-Vigneau, both still producing wine of high quality.

It is in the parish of Sauternes itself, however, that the greatest sweet white wine in the world is made. Today, a century after Château d'Yquem was crowned as the *Premier Grand Cru*, it is still pre-eminent. Its wine is made from grapes which are so overripe as to be almost mouldy (with the *pourriture noble* upon them), and are carefully selected one by one. Each grape yields but a few drops of luscious juice, and the most meticulous attention is devoted to every detail in the long process of wine making. The colour of Yquem is golden, the bouquet almost overpowering in its perfumed strength, and the flavour is a revelation of what the nectar of the gods might be, full of the very essence of sweetness. Other vineyards in the district make splendid wines—Château Rieussec, Château Lafaurie-Peyraguey, Château Guiraud and others—but none seriously challenges the greatness of Château d'Yquem. Seize upon any opportunity offered to taste this wine, particularly of a fine vintage year. 1961 was outstanding, and there is a range of good wines back to 1921. It will be an experience never to be forgotten.

🐘 🐘 🐘

SAUTERNES AND BARSAC
Premier Grand Cru

CH. D'YQUEM	SAUTERNES

Premiers Crus

CH. LA TOUR-BLANCHE	BOMMES
CH. LAFAURIE-PEYRAGUEY	BOMMES
CH. CLOS HAUT-PEYRAGUEY	BOMMES
CH. DE RAYNE-VIGNEAU	BOMMES
CH. DE SUDUIRAUT	PREIGNAC
CH. COUTET	BARSAC
CH. CLIMENS	BARSAC
CH. GUIRAUD	SAUTERNES
CH. RIEUSSEC	FARGUES
CH. RABAUD-PROMIS	BOMMES
CH. SIGALAS-RABAUD	BOMMES

Deuxièmes Crus

CH. MYRAT	BARSAC
CH. DOISY-DUBROCA	BARSAC
CH. DOISY-DAËNE	BARSAC
CH. DOISY-VÉDRINES	BARSAC
CH. D'ARCHE	SAUTERNES
CH. D'ARCHE LAFAURIE	SAUTERNES
CH. FILHOT	SAUTERNES
CH. BROUSTET	BARSAC
CH. NAIRAC	BARSAC
CH. CAILLOU	BARSAC
CH. SUAU	BARSAC
CH. DE MALLE	PREIGNAC
CH. ROMER	FARGUES
CH. LAMOTHE	SAUTERNES

SOME VINTAGES OF BORDEAUX WHITE WINES SINCE 1955

1955	Very good	1964	Very good
1957	Good average	1966	Very good
1959	Very good	1967	Good
1960	Good	1969	Good
1961	Excellent	1970	Excellent
1962	Very good	1971	Good

The above are regarded as the best vintage years, but in some vineyards good wines were made in many years of less renown. Editor.

II · BURGUNDY

BY H. WARNER ALLEN

How to choose Burgundy! The solution of the problem is far from easy. For few wines is the guidance offered by the label less adequate. If you choose a Claret, say Château Latour 1929, you know the kind of wine you are ordering, though the conditions of its keeping and so on will distinguish one bottle from another. But if you call for a Burgundy, say Chambertin 1955, the wine may turn out to be superlatively good, moderate, or inferior. And for the beginner the best way to get over this difficulty is to shift the burden to the shoulders of the professional expert.

A wine-lover ordering for his own cellar can, if he takes the trouble, enter into personal relations with a wine merchant, a wine-lover like himself, who has studied conscientiously from A to Z the history of the wares he sells. Hospitality is the watchword of the profession, and by the wines he drinks you may judge your wine merchant. He should be a master, not only of salesmanship like a grocer, and of the treatment of wine in the country where he sells it (like a retailer of beer), but also of the whole complicated process which culminates in the bottling of the vineyard sunshine and of the art of vinous appreciation.

What of Burgundy in restaurants? May I venture to suggest that not all waiters are to be trusted? And, unfortunately, it is only on occasions that the name of the firm responsible for the wine is mentioned on the wine list.

If the wine flies no flag of a reputed shipper, there remain as identifying marks the vintage years, which are of peculiar importance in the choice between unknown Burgundies. In most wine districts, more especially in the Gironde, the climate is so favourable to the vine that it is exceedingly rare that some good wine is not made somewhere in the region, however bad the year. Burgundy lies so far to the north that, when conditions are unfavourable, the wine-grower has to resort to expedients, perfectly legitimate in the circumstances, but unfortunate for the quality of the wine, to save it from a premature death.

He often has to heat the must to encourage fermentation and so incurs the reproach of his rival, the Bordelais, who will have it quite unfairly that all Burgundy tastes of the cooked grape. Unripe grapes are so grudging in the sugar, which is the measure of alcohol in the wine, that their fermented juice will come to an untimely end. If the wine is to be saved, cane sugar must be added to the must in quantity sufficient to raise the alcoholic degree to a point high enough to give the finished product stability. The process, called *chaptalisation*, from the great chemist Chaptal who discovered it, destroys the finer points of bouquet and aroma and leaves a dull, uninspiring beverage. In a good year, when the must is pressed from fully ripe grapes, the wine-grower's need to add sugar is reduced to a minimum, since he can depend on the sugar in the fruit. There is an easy mnemonic for most of the best Burgundy years. Since 1906 they have almost all been odd numbers.

Finest of all: 1911, 1915, 1923, 1929, 1945, 1947, 1953, 1955, 1957, 1959, 1961.

Next best: 1919, 1921, 1933, 1937, 1943, 1949, with the even numbers, 1926, 1934, 1948 and 1952 as exceptions.

For another reason, the choice of an unknown Burgundy on the strength of a label or name on the wine list is always a leap in the dark, apart from the guarantee of a good shipper. Burgundy is a land of small—extremely small—holdings, and wine-growers own little patches consisting of a few rows of vines scattered all over the district. (These small proprietors doubled in number in the five years after World War II.) Mass-production robs wine of its birthright, but in Burgundy the making of wine has gone so far to the opposite extreme that it is in danger of producing its opposite.

To take an example, the whole of Clos de Vougeot, a hundred and twenty-five acres, the largest vineyard of the Côte de Nuits, was once the property of the Cistercians, who made there three *cuvées*: the one from the top slopes too precious to be sold, the second from the mid-slopes still of superlative quality, and the third from the lower slopes which ranked among the finest wines of the region. The Revolution put an end to this happy state of affairs, and after many vicissitudes the famous vineyard has been split up between more than forty smallholders. Each owner of a patch of vines has his own ideas as to the making of wine, and consequently each year the vineyard produces a number of different wines, varying in quality with the skill and conscientiousness of their makers. It is not surprising that there is a tendency for certain firms to follow the example set by Champagne and to produce *monopoles* guaranteed of standard quality in which, through blending, the charm of local distinctions is lost.

Happily, however, the best dealers in wine still preserve the ancient traditions, and the prestige of the great Burgundy names remains intact. The Côte d'Or, the slopes golden in autumn with the turning vine leaves, and golden for the value of their harvest, is divided midway into two parts; on the north the Côte de Nuits, on the south the Côte de Beaune.

The grandest of all Burgundies, of the rarest bouquet, the most velvety texture and the richest aroma, are grown in the Côte de Nuits. Traversing it from north to south, we find the parish of Gevrey with Chambertin, the wine beloved by Napoleon Bonaparte, and Clos de Bèze; then Morey with Clos de Tart, Chambolle with Musigny, lightest and most fragrant of its kind, Gilly with Clos de Vougeot, which has sometimes surpassed the greatest wines of the Côte d'Or; and Flagey with Les Grands Echézeaux, very fine wine which is said to be handicapped in Britain by what is regarded as the outlandishness of its name. There follows Vosne, the apple of the eye of every Burgundy lover, with the vineyards of Romanée-Conti, a few acres which have for centuries been held peerless for the perfection of their wine, recently lying fallow and waiting to be planted with grafted stock proof against phylloxera; La Romanée, Les Richebourgs, La Tâche and La Romanée-Saint-Vivant. Vosne is to Burgundy what Pauillac is to the Médoc, a cluster of the very finest vineyards in the whole region. The Côte de Nuits ends with the little town which gives it its name, renowned for the vines of Saint-Georges.

The Côte de Beaune begins with the most famous of its *communes*, Aloxe, with the vineyards of Le Corton and Clos du Roi. Beaune itself has been reputed for its wines for centuries, and the Hospices de Beaune, ever memorable for the annual wine auction, owns many of the vineyards of the Côte. Pommard and Volnay often produce excellent wines, though rarely, if ever, rising to the heights of the wines of the Côte de Nuits.

Striking south from the Côte de Beaune we come to the Côte Chalonnaise, with the excellent wine of Mercurey. It is grown from the Pinot grape, like the great wines of the Côte d'Or, but magnificence has given place to qualities less rare.

Mercurey is a wine to be drunk young in big bumpers with little more than a superficial analysis of its pleasant charm.

Still farther south, where the Mâconnais and Beaujolais meet, the Gamay grape, which in the Côte d'Or gives quantity and no quality, becomes a reformed character and produces wines less dignified and with less breed than the Pinot-grown wines of Mercurey, but refreshing, agreeable wines to be quaffed without stint and undue thought. In good years they keep well, but age brings them little improvement, and I prefer them at cellar temperature. Good wines are grown in the *commune* of Romanêche-Thorins, just within the boundary of the Mâconnais but listed with the wines of Beaujolais, and we have, among others, Moulin à Vent, Morgon, Brouilly, and the vineyards at Fleurie, Juliénas and Chénas.

What is the difference, it may be asked, between a wine bearing the name of Beaujolais and those other wines called Moulin à Vent, etc., which are the names of vineyards in the Beaujolais district? This can be simply explained. In 1935 the National Committee for regulating the place-names of wine and Brandy set to work. It is now illegal to give a wine the name of a territory or vineyard where the grapes were not grown, and the wines must be made from the fruit of specifically named vines. Moreover, to have the right to vineyard names the wines must have a minimum alcoholic strength and quantity of sugar. Supposing one year that a Moulin à Vent turns out to have a strength of under 10 per cent of alcohol, it must be named only "Beaujolais." If the wine of the famous vineyard Clos de Vougeot should by some mischance turn out to have an alcoholic content of less than 12 per cent it must take one step down and be named only "Vougeot"; and if by an even greater misfortune the strength should be under 10·5 per cent the wine must be demoted still further and be named simply "Bourgogne." Similar rules apply to the content of sugar in the wine. Let it be clearly understood that this law does not govern bouquet or flavour, or indeed any of the finer aesthetic qualities of a wine; but at least the buyer does know what he is getting so far as alcohol and sugar are concerned.

If I were pressed to name what I consider the finest of all Burgundies I should find it difficult to depart very far from the list drawn up by M. Brunet, a man whose opinion must be respected, and I should name as the Grand First Growths the following: Romanée Conti (in the parish of Vosne), Clos de Vougeot (Vougeot), La Tâche (Vosne), Richebourg (Vosne), La Romanée (Vosne), Chambertin (Gevrey), Musigny (Chambolle), Le Clos de Tart (Morey), Corton (Aloxe), Saint-Georges (Nuits). And following close behind: Les Bonnes Mares (Morey), Les Lambrays (Morey), Romanée Saint-Vivant (Vosne), Clos de Bèze (Gevrey), Les Grands Echézeaux (Flagey).

Let us pass from the choice to the enjoyment of Burgundy. It is necessary for the serious consideration of any wine to know what one should look for as its special characteristic. The sources of pleasure may be defined as colour, bouquet, and taste, or "aroma," when the wine is held in the mouth and in point of fact is smelt rather than tasted.

As to colour, no wine appeals to the eye more magnificently than Burgundy. The cruder reds and purples of a young Burgundy should weather with age into a profundity of colour. When a fine old wine is washed round the glass the rich purple hue of the depths, like the transparent glow of a rare ruby, shades off into a dark garnet red in its shallower ripples, passing into the legendary *pelure d'oignon,* where only a thin film of wine touches the glass. I must confess that I know very little about the peeling of onions, and I cannot remember any formal definition of this onion tint which is a special characteristic of fine ancient Burgundy and is present with equal intensity only in the Rhône wines, but I have always taken it to apply to the golden sheen which seems to glint through the purples of the liquid when in rotation. When in the Odyssey the unrecognized Odysseus is describing to Penelope the clothes he wore on a certain occasion, he tells of a purple cloak and about the body a tunic, "shining like the peel of a dry onion—so soft it was and it glistened like the sun." Purple and gold meet in the onion with its smooth and bright golden sheath and touches of deep colour in its inner layers.

The bouquet of a fine Burgundy is, I think, a better guide to its all-round merits than that of any other natural wine. It is exceedingly rare that a Burgundy which has pleased the nose disappoints the palate, though in other old wines an exceptionally delightful bouquet may herald an aroma which has faded or the all-too-dry finish of senility. The Greeks had a wine which, when the jar was opened, filled the house with the scent of roses, violets and hyacinths. The bouquet of a great Burgundy is more privately and discreetly exclusive. It is content to embalm the interior of the glass, and thence the nose, with a concentration of perfume. "An unanalysable *je ne sais quoi* compounded of the suavity of a thousand scents"— so one might describe this bouquet with the lame and prosaic version of a traitorous translator of Dante's *Purgatorio*, which tells of the great ones of the earth waiting to expiate their sins in a valley where Nature *"di soavità di mille odori . . . faceva un incognito indistinto."*

In the mouth, too, Burgundy boasts a distinction all its own. Its supreme quality may perhaps reside in the sensation arising from its contact with tongue and palate and culminating at the moment of swallowing. An eighteenth-century Romanée-Conti served at the table of the Archbishop of Paris called forth the exclamation: "Bottled satin añd velvet!" I know no other wine which is so caressingly suave in its tactile quality. Certain liqueurs and the very rich dessert wines which the French call *liquoreux* are exceedingly luscious and smooth. They glide like a kiss over the tongue and palate with the suavity of oil or glycerine, and sometimes leave behind them a film of intense sweetness. Walter Berry said of one of the Midi Muscat wines: "Their sweetness sticks to the lips, prolonging the pleasure of taste like a lingering kiss." I do not share his affection for sticky kisses; and there is nothing sticky, nothing cloying, in the caress of a fine Burgundy. Its satin and velvet transcend mere lifeless materials; but as it is itself a living thing, so its softness has something of the thrill of living flesh. To make the most of this sensation, the very essence of the enjoyment of Burgundy, there must be no hurry, no hasty gulping down of the wine. It must be held pursed up in the mouth, until it has embalmed every approach to the private universe of sensation.

❧ ❧ ❧

THE WHITE WINES OF BURGUNDY

The vineyards of Chablis lie in Lower Burgundy in the Department of the Yonne, and though they are over a hundred miles north-west of the Côte d'Or their wines are counted among the Burgundies. These white wines, delicate and light, are of the most attractive character and excel as the perfect heralds of other more imposing wines, as they prepare the palate most agreeably and leave nothing behind that can interfere with the appreciation of the most subtle shades of bouquet and aroma.

They are a perfect accompaniment for oysters, should be drunk cold, and much should be made of their bouquet. I know of no wine paler in colour—light topaz tinged with the faintest hint of green. There has been much legal controversy as to the true definition of the term Chablis, and the vineyards have been divided into three sections: Grand Chablis with the finest *crus*; Chablis with the next-best growths, also called Lignorelles; and ordinary Bourgogne des Environs de Chablis. In no wine is an admixture of sugar more deadly than in the case of Chablis; for its charm depends on its unsophisticated freshness as the driest of all wines. All the best vineyards—the white Pinot or Chardonnay is the Chablis grape—are planted on the right bank of the River Serein, and among the finest growths rank Vaudésir, Valmur, Les Clos, Les Grenouilles, Les Preuses, Mont de Milieu, Les Fourchaumes and Moutonne.

The same grape, the Chardonnay, is responsible for the greatest wine of the Côte de Beaune whether red or white, the greatest of all Burgundy white wines, and one of the greatest white wines in the world, Montrachet. Puligny and Chassagne divide the honour of being the home of Montrachet, a dry wine of great splendour and strength, which from time to time embarrasses its shippers by exceeding the alcohol degree of the lower scale of duties for natural wines. The Marquis de la Guiche and Baron Thénard are the chief proprietors of the vineyards which have the right to style their wines Montrachet with no qualification, only eight acres in all. Professor Saintsbury called it "a magnificent and formidable wine" and spoke of it making one's veins swell like whipcord. I admit that its volume of taste is tremendous, but it has never had any untoward effects on my veins. The finest Montrachet I ever tasted came from the Marquis de la Guiche's vineyard in the 1889 vintage, and in its old age its bouquet was marvellous. Chevalier Montrachet and Bâtard Montrachet are excellent wines grown above and below their peerless namesake.

Meursault, another denizen of the Côte de Beaune, ranks as one of the best-known white Burgundies and it has considerable merit, though to my palate there is a touch of coarseness in its special tang which makes it one of the easiest wines to recognize. Its best vineyards are Perrières, Genevrières and Charmes, though the best Meursault I ever tasted was grown in the Goutte d'Or vineyard in 1911.

At the other end of the Côte de Beaune, at Aloxe, Corton Blanc must be added to the white wines of the region. Its grapes are grown in the Charlemagne vineyard which stretches round the curve of the Corton Hill into the *commune* of Pernand, and is said to have belonged to the great Emperor. It is a sound, agreeable wine, but I find many of these white Burgundies, exception being made for Montrachet and Chablis, rather lacking in character and delicacy. Some white wine is still made at Clos de Vougeot.

Our survey of the white wines of Burgundy comes to an end

with those of the Mâconnais, which are derived from Pouilly and part of the *communes* of Fuissé, Solutré and Chaintré, usually known as Pouilly or Pouilly-Fuissé and to be distinguished from the *blanc-fumé* wines of Pouilly-sur-Loire. They are made from the Chardonnay and differ from all other Burgundy white wines in taking advantage of the *Botrytis cinerea* or "noble mould" which is responsible for the intense and luscious sweetness of Sauternes. The grapes ripe in September are left on the vines, perhaps till November, when the mould has concentrated their sugar. The Chardonnay gives a wine far less rich than the grapes of Sauternes, but one which is very fruity, of a deep golden colour and not over-sweet. It is ready to drink after four or five years, and lacks the coarseness which is to be remarked in the lesser white Burgundies of the Côte d'Or.

❧ ❧ ❧

RED BURGUNDY VINTAGES SINCE 1943

1943	Good	1959	Very good
1945	Very good	1960	Average quality
1947	Exceptionally good	1961	Excellent
1948	Good	1962	Light but very good
1949	Very good	1964	Excellent
1950	Fair	1966	Excellent
1952	Well balanced wines	1967	Many good wines
1953	Light and elegant	1969	Excellent
1955	Some outstanding wines	1970	Very good
1957	Many good wines	1971	Small but good vintage

III · CHAMPAGNE

BY ANDRÉ L. SIMON

CHAMPAGNE is the best of all wines—at times. There is no wine that is the best all the time: so much depends upon not only our taste but our mood, upon conditions, circumstances and the company. Let us imagine, for instance, that we are having lunch at Ascot or Goodwood. The choice is lobster salad or cold Scotch salmon; you have the one and I have the other, but we both will call for Champagne, because Champagne is the best wine we can possibly think of. Claret or Burgundy would be entirely out of place, and Vintage Port quite unthinkable. Now imagine that you back losers consistently for the first three races: it is just a supposition, but it has happened to me and it may one day happen to you. And go on supposing a little further: suppose that in sheer desperation you put your shirt on the outsider with the longest odds in the 3.30, and it romps home. Your wife may be with you, or it may be your best

friend's best wife: it makes no difference: you must celebrate:
you must have the best. Are you going to call for a bottle
of Château Latour 1929, or Les Grands Echézeaux 1923,
or Cockburn '08? They all are great wines, and you and I
could write whole books about them, describing their
bouquet, body and breed, yet at the moment you would not
have any one of them as a gift: what you want is Champagne, and no other wine would be acceptable.

Champagne is not the only wine with bubbles in it, but
it is the best of all sparkling wines. It is the best simply
because it is made of better grapes and with greater care
than the rest. It is said that from the man who picks the
grapes which are to be pressed to make Champagne, to
the one who will wrap it up for dispatch, after it has been
finally given its label and foil, each bottle of Champagne
passes through one hundred different pairs of hands.

This gives some idea of the infinite care necessary to
bring a bottle of Champagne to the remarkable degree of
perfection which justifies its high price. But, costly as all
this nursing may be, it is responsible for the fact that
Champagne is better able than any other wine to stand the
trials and shocks of life.

Just think of it. A bottle of Champagne has spent some
years, never less than three and often as long as ten, in the
cool peace of its Reims, Ay or Épernay cellar, many feet deep
down into the quarried chalk. Then the "call" comes; it is
hauled up to the light of day, washed, dressed up with
label and foil, wrapped up in coloured tissue-paper, cased
and sent by rail to Antwerp, Havre or any other port. It
may be the depth of winter; it will be left overnight on the
quayside whatever the frost or snow may be; then it will
be flung down the hold of the steamer, which will carry it,
shaking, throbbing, pulsating and rocking all the time,
through the hell of the Red Sea to the still hotter hell of
the concrete quays of Mombasa, before it has another
thorough shaking on its way up by train to Nairobi. There

it may have a rest under the stifling tin roof of some wine
stores, until at long last somebody with a thirst and a purse
gets hold of it, sticks it hard into a bucket of crushed ice,
leaves it there for an hour or so. And after all this, when the
cork is set free and the wine is poured out, it bubbles out
as clear as crystal, crisp, fresh, delicious, all smiles, as if
everybody had been kind to it all along. Is it not wonderful?
Of course it is, and there is no other wine that can stand
what Champagne can stand.

If by now you believe, as I do myself, that Champagne
is really a wonderful wine, you might like to know where it
comes from and how it is made.

The Champagne country lies due east of Paris, south-
west and west of the Ardennes and Vosges Mountains, its
far from effective natural defences against the Hunnish
hordes out of Tartary long ago, and the mechanized hordes
out of Germany in more modern times. La Champagne is
mostly flat and drab; its great plains and its few hunched-up
sets of hills are in turn swept by icy winds from the east
during the winter, and scorched by merciless heat during
the summer. It has but one fair river, the historic River
Marne. The soil of La Champagne is light and poor, without any depth of humus upon a subsoil of white chalk.
Where a range of hills rises between Reims and Épernay
the soil is no richer, but it has proved none the less highly
suitable for wine-making grapes during the past fifteen
hundred years—or two thousand years if we agree that the
Romans were the first to plant grapes where dense forests
had flourished before their advent.

Today the vineyards of La Champagne grace the slopes
of two opposite ranges of hills of the Valley of the Marne,
above and below Épernay. In the more important of the two,
La Montagne de Reims, some 80 per cent of the grapes
grown are black Pinot grapes, and 20 per cent white Pinot.
In the Montagne d'Avize white Pinot grapes are grown
almost exclusively. The Pinot, whether black or white, is

one of the great aristocrats, making wines which have that most elusive and attractive of all wine-virtues called, for lack of a better word, *breed*. But one must not forget that it is entirely due to hard work, the only hard currency which Nature accepts, that the poor, chalky soil of La Champagne's vineyards has been made to yield, in the course of the centuries, a wine of such unique excellence and appeal that it has been—and still is—the source of wealth beyond the dreams of avarice.

Champagne was not always a sparkling wine: for hundreds of years it was a table wine, red if made of black grapes, white if made of white grapes. Sparkling Champagne was first heard of at the end of the seventeenth century; but up to about one hundred years ago sparkling Champagne was the exception, and red still Champagne was the rule. Dom Pérignon has been hailed as the inventor or creator of sparkling Champagne, but he never claimed to have been anything of the sort, nor did any of his contemporaries (he lived from 1639 to 1715) claim any such honour for him. All who knew him praised his kindly disposition and professional ability: "He loved the poor and he made excellent wine." Dom Pérignon, Cellarer of the Abbey of Hautvillers, never wished for a better epitaph: he would certainly have resented being hailed as the first man to have "put bubbles into Champagne," when neither he nor anybody else ever put bubbles into Champagne.

The bubbles of sparkling Champagne are the same as the bubbles of bottled beer: they are tiny drops of liquid disturbed, whipped and chased by escaping carbonic-acid gas at the time of fermentation. If we want our wine to be sparkling, all we have to do is to prevent the carbonic-acid gas from escaping into the air. We must bottle it up; cork it up, and make sure that the cork is tightly and safely wired or tied so that the gas inside the bottle cannot push it out. That is where Dom Pérignon comes in. He was the first to use stoppers made of cork bark in place of the wads of hemp that were used at that time to keep dust and dirt out of the wine; sometimes just a drop of olive oil was used, for bottles of wine were always kept standing upright and never for any length of time. Sparkling wine, and also still wine matured in bottle, did not and could not exist in France before stoppers made of cork bark were imported from Spain.

Today, as soon as the grapes grown in the vineyards of La Champagne are ripe they are picked and brought in small baskets to the nearest roadside to be spread upon large osier trays and looked over, bunch by bunch, by a number of sharp-eyed, expert old women, armed with long, pointed scissors, who remove unsound, unripe or otherwise defective berries. The bunches are piled in great baskets, loaded on cart or van, and delivered with the least possible delay to the nearest *vendangeoir,* and are weighed and tipped into the *pressoir,* a square oak press holding four tons of grapes. When the heavy oak lid is brought down upon the mass of grapes in the press they are crushed and their sweet juice runs down a wide groove into a large vat on the floor below.

The grapes may be black grapes or white: it does not really make much—if any—difference to the colour of the wine. The juice of black Pinot grapes is greenish white, and the colouring pigment lies inside the lining of the black grapes' skins. To make red wine, the white juice must be allowed to lie and ferment in contact with the black-red skins of the grapes; but if we want to make white wine from black grapes, as we do in Champagne, the white juice is allowed to run at once into a vat where the black skins will never be admitted.

Let us keep our eye on those four hundred and fifty gallons of white grape-juice in the vat. Bubbles begin to appear on the surface. The grape-juice frets; it gets hot; it throws up a froth, discarding the dust and dirt that came in with the grapes. It is fermenting. As a matter of fact, it has now ceased to be grape-juice at all; some of its grape-sugar has already escaped as carbon dioxide and some has become alcohol, which means that we have now wine instead of grape-juice in our vat. So we promptly draw our very new wine into ten casks, each holding forty-four gallons, for the original four hundred and fifty have lost ten gallons in the course of fermentation.

The casks of new wine are sent usually by motor lorries to the cellars of their owner, be he an individual *vigneron* or one of the great shipping Houses, and they are left more or less alone for the next six months or so. This gives the wine a chance to go on fermenting very slowly and to settle down sufficiently for the *Chef de Cave* to taste it critically and to make up his mind how best to "assemble" or blend his various *cuvées*.

Every great House has large reserves of wines made in the best vintage years, wines which are kept in casks to be blended with the new wine of later and less favoured years, in order to raise their standard of quality. When the *Chef de Cave*, after many careful tastings and trials, is satisfied that his *cuvée*, the wine of the year, is worthy of the reputation of the House whose name it will bear on its label in years to come, his next problem is to make sure that, when the time comes to offer this *cuvée* for sale, the wine shall be sparkling, and with neither too much nor too little carbonic-acid gas in it. This means (1) that the wine must be bottled; (2) that it must be securely corked so that no gas from within can push the cork out; and (3) that, on bottling, just the right amount of sugar is added to produce just the right amount of gas: too little would result in flat Champagne, which is dull; too much would burst the bottles, which is worse.

And it must now be left alone, stacked in great piles of many thousands of bottles, in deep, cold cellars cut out of the chalk rock, and given a chance to transform through fermentation every bit of the sugar there is in it into alcohol and carbon dioxide. But a sediment, the inevitable discard of all fermented wines, will form—and it is a tricky job to remove this.

When the bottles are lifted from their stacks they are stuck into specially made grids or racks, head or cork first, with their punt slightly tilted up. Every other day a *remueur* or "shaker," a man with strong hands and a light touch, seizes each bottle, gives it a few rotating tremors, and pushes it forward just enough to leave the punt tilted a little higher. Thus the sediment inside the bottle is made to slide down a little nearer the cork, until, in the end, the bottle is standing practically on its head, or rather on its cork. Now comes the *dégorgeur* to release the clamp that holds the cork in the bottle and let the gas blow out the cork together with all the sediment now packed upon its inside face. His skill is such that hardly any wine and bubbles escape. Nowadays a refrigerating machine, devised to freeze hard that one inch of dirty Champagne with all the sediment in it, makes it safer and quicker to remove the cork with the small lump of frozen wine-cum-dirt stuck to it, leaving the rest of the wine in the bottle absolutely star-bright.

Now is the time to settle a very important question: "Is the wine in the bottle too dry?" The answer depends entirely upon the taste of the people who will eventually be drinking it: sweeter for the French, who drink Champagne at the end of the meal with *gâteaux* and *dessert*, and drier for the great majority of the English, who enjoy it before a meal, or with fish and white meats. To make sure that he will have some Champagne to please all and sundry, the *Chef de Cave* adds 5 per cent, 3 per cent, 2 per cent, 1 per cent, ½ per cent or ¼ per cent of sweet *liqueur* to different wines, after the sediment has been removed and before the second and last cork is forced in and securely wired on.

The wine is given a few weeks' rest to assimilate the sugar, and it may then be sold. But there is no hurry; on the contrary, there is much to be gained by leaving the wine alone for another year, maybe two or even three: it will gain in quality by losing some of its original acidity.

Champagne bottles are more smartly dressed than most, if

not all, other wine bottles. Besides its foil, which gives it a
festive appearance, it bears one or more "labels," or notices,
each conveying some item of information: the name of the
Shipper, and maybe his badge, crest or trade-mark; the House
responsible for the wine; the date of the Vintage (that is if the
whole or most of the wine was made from grapes picked and
pressed in a single year); an indication of how sweet or dry the
wine may be, either *Sec,* which (applied to Champagne) means
sweet; *Demi Sec,* which means sweeter; *Extra Sec* or *Extra
Dry,* which means drier; *Brut* or *Nature,* which should mean a
wholly unsweetened wine; the Royal Arms, which means that
the Shipper holds the Royal Warrant and that his Champagne
has been supplied to the Royal Cellars; sometimes the *cuvée*
is described on a label as *Special* or *Réservée.* Anything else
that is likely to be useful or ornamental can be found a place
on some label stuck high or low on the Champagne bottle.
Thus when Messrs. Moët et Chandon, in the year of King
Edward VII's Coronation, shipped their Vintage of 1898, the
King's head appeared on the label, in gold, the size of a penny.

Champagne should always be served cold, but not over-
iced. Too cold, too sweet or too much Champagne overnight
means an unholy thirst the morning after, but no headache.

When the wire which holds the Champagne cork in place
is removed the bottle should be held in a slanting position so
that the wine and its gas do not rush out madly as soon as the
cork is released, which they will do if the bottle be held
vertically.

As soon as the cork is out, pour a little wine into a glass and
bring it to the tribunal of your nose. Smell it with care to be
sure that the wine is free from the taint of a mouldy cork or
any other possible blemish. Should you detect the least objectionable smell, there is nothing else to do but get another
bottle.

It is important to make sure that Champagne is served in
well-polished glasses: when glasses are at all damp, the
Champagne bubbles will rise in a sluggish instead of a lively

manner. To beat the bubbles out with a "mosser" or a fork is sheer waste of money and good wine: anybody with a diaphragm allergic to bubbles had very much better order a still wine.

Champagne usually has a golden straw colour. But there is also some Champagne which is made pink, and it may match the pink-silk shades of your candles: it is neither better nor worse than golden Champagne.

Vintage Champagne is, by definition, the wine of one and the same year or vintage, a year when the grapes were perfectly ripe and sound. In practice, however, when the demand for a very popular brand is greater than the supply, or it may be for economic considerations, a Vintage Champagne can be a blend of wines, a large proportion of the blend being from grapes gathered in the year which appears on the cork and label, whilst a smaller proportion is made up of usually less expensive wines of former vintages.

Any Champagne which is sold without the date of a particular vintage may be safely considered to be a blend of the wines of different years: such a wine is always cheaper than the dated wines, although it is sometimes very good indeed and may well be better value than many a dated Vintage.

There was no lack of sunshine during the war summers of 1941, 1942, 1943, and wines of all three years were shipped as Vintage wine by various Champagne shippers. If one remembers that when the wines of those three vintages were due to be bottled (1942, 1943, 1944) France was occupied by the Germans, it is quite remarkable that they were so good when shipped to Britain after the war. The lack of skilled labour and the shortage of new Champagne bottles and first-quality Spanish corks must have made it particularly difficult for the Champagne shippers.

The 1945 and 1947 Vintage Champagnes were rightly hailed as very good; and those of 1952, 1953 and 1955, as well as several later ones, came up to a good standard.

At mealtime, dry Champagne is excellent with hors-d'oeuvre, fish, entrées and all white meats, but it is also most acceptable throughout the whole meal.

Champagne is the best wine, as a matter of fact the only wine, one can enjoy last thing at night and first thing in the morning; at a ball in the early hours of the morning—and at eleven o'clock the same morning when a gentle pick-me-up is so very, very welcome!

🐚 🐚 🐚

SOME CHAMPAGNE VINTAGES

The vintages in 1945 and 1947 were very good, and in 1946, 1949, 1952, 1953 and 1955 they maintained a good average.

The long hot summer of 1959 produced rather dark heavy wines; most firms shipped them.

In 1961, good and well-balanced wines were made, lighter than those of 1959.

In 1962, wines were light and attractive, but not generally up to the standard of the 1961s.

In 1964, there were fine well-balanced wines which have fully realized all expectations.

In 1966 the wines were light, elegant and charming.

IV · WINES OF GERMANY

BY ALFRED LANGENBACH

FINE wine can best be appreciated only by those who have learned to enjoy it for its finesse in bouquet and character, not for its body and lusciousness. This may sound strange, but after all it is *breed* which decides the value of wine, as it does, say, that of horses, dogs, cattle—or indeed any living being. Only thus does wine-drinking become a delight, and only thus is it raised to an inspiring and elevating pleasure high above the consumption of other alcoholic drinks.

The bouquet is the result of various organisms which can be separated into two totally different kinds. The one is the grape-bouquet derived from certain organic substances in the grapes, and developed with the fermentation; the other grows in bottle from totally different origins at a time when the grape-bouquet is slowly receding. Red wines will profit more from the bottle-bouquet, which in particular distinguishes those lovely Médoc wines or the fine Rheingau, and which therefore also need a longer bottle age. On the other hand,

¹ Mr. Langenbach prefers to use the names Rhine wine and Mosel wine for what are more commonly known in Britain as Hock and Moselle. Hock is, of course, a name of doubtful pedigree, and Moselle is the name only of that section of the river which flows on the French side of the frontier. *Editor.*

many of the white wines are particularly pleasant as long as the grape-bouquet prevails; for example, Mosel wines.

In both kinds the bouquet takes its character from the vines, and is the result of the type of vine planted. You can easily recognize the similarity by tasting the grape and then tasting the wine made from the same grapes.

The main types of vine grown in Germany for the production of white wines are the Sylvaner (also called Oesterreicher, as it comes from Austria) and the Riesling, besides which we will only mention the Gutedel, Kleinberger and the Traminer; but of all these species there are many varieties and many crossings. Whilst the Sylvaner bears fleshy and juicy grapes and yields good quantities, the Riesling produces small but very tasty grapes and gives a smaller output. Various types of vine blossom at various stages, some sooner, some later, and their grapes in the same way mature in the early autumn or later. The choice of the species of vine will therefore have to be made also subject to the risks of late frosts in the spring and early frosts in the autumn—factors of particular importance in German vineyards, the most northerly in Europe.

Wines grown in near proximity can produce very different results. You will sometimes see pictured "Father Rhine" together with his daughter "Mosella." We can hereby gain an idea also of the principal distinctions of their wines: the Rhine wine masculine, with body and full flavour, possibly also great richness; the Mosel, slim, light and elegant, with a delicate yet very distinct grape-bouquet and even a slight and savoury acid finish. The colour will generally be somewhat deeper with the Rhine than with the Mosel wine; we should, however, abstain from considering this as a distinctive characteristic. All depends upon the ripeness of the grapes at harvest-time, for the colour is gained from the skin of the grapes and increases with maturity. It can further increase when the grapes or the "must"—the product after the pressing of the grapes —has been exposed to the air, a procedure which one prefers to avoid nowadays.

These remarks apply to white wines of the Rhine and Mosel areas. Most German red wines are consumed within the country and are rarely of interest for export. Whilst the difference in bouquet and taste between the white Rhine and Mosel wines is very marked, it is not so easy to recognize differences between those of the various districts of the Rhine. We reckon principally in this area—starting from the south—the Palatinate, Rhenish Hessia, the Rheingau and the Nahe.

The vineyards of the Palatinate—in German called "Pfalz" or "Rheinpfalz"—enjoy a southerly climate, and produce therefore the ripest of all German wines, tender and well balanced. Even the ordinary wines, with a reasonably good vintage, will become mellow, with a distinct though somewhat coarse bouquet. Those of the higher class in the middle Palatinate show abundance of aroma, body and flavour, and the best growths in fine vintages attain a delightful sweetness combined with richness of bouquet.

The best of Rhenish Hessia can come very near to this achievement, though the average wine is of a less pronounced, quieter style, yet indeed with a delightful and soft flavour, which also makes the cheaper of its products attractive.

The Rheingau take an almost individual status, where Riesling is predominant, and if you can spare them a couple of years in bottle even the most modest will satisfy you by its charming though reticent bouquet and character. The finest will deserve the title of kings of all white wines by their firmness, their great yet unobtrusive sweetness, their noble and quite outstanding lilac-like aroma.

Their sisters of the Nahe take position between Rhine and Mosel. The ordinary wines are somewhat similar to those of Rhenish Hessia, but the Rieslings grown on rocks gain in good years a quite outstanding bouquet and elegance, and thereby remind one in many ways of high-class Mosel.

Whilst Mosel wines, as already explained, have a pronounced character of their own, they vary considerably amongst themselves. The majority are light, stimulating, dry wines, which can well be consumed without a meal; there is indeed no better appetizer than a bottle of ordinary Mosel instead of cocktails, and it also leads well up to any other wine, white or red, when given at the start of the meal. Those of moderate quality are best drunk young, when you imagine still the scent of the grape, and enjoy them, properly cooled, as a most refreshing beverage. They frequently retain a slight amount of carbonic-acid gas, when they are described as being *spritzig*. They have a prickle, which is a residue of fermentation and keeps the wine fresh.

Excellent wines are grown on the middle Mosel—between Trier and Enkirch or Reil—and equally so on the Rivers Saar and Ruhr. Indeed, these two tributaries of the Mosel often produce wines of greater bouquet, though the wines are of a more delicate nature.

All these wines should be served at a cool temperature, in summer even iced if a refrigerator is not available. It must be borne in mind that the bouquet of wine disappears, or at least diminishes, when the temperature of the wine is too low or too high. This first will be remedied quickly in the warm room, or adjust itself quite naturally in summer; too warm a temperature, however, is almost irreparable. For white wines 45 deg. to 50 deg. F. is correct. Too high a temperature disrupts the taste, as both acidity and sweetness appear out of proportion.

Do not decant German wines, but wherever possible have the corks drawn some little while before consumption. Have good-sized, white glasses, and do not fill them more than three-quarters so that you can let the wine rotate in the glass, thus giving it a chance to open up and display its aroma to advantage. Whilst a wine should be bright in appearance, slight crusty sediments are the natural secretion of tartaric acids caused by a process which indeed improves the quality of the wine. If you give the bottle a chance to stand for a short while, these deposits will settle at the bottom and will hardly become noticeable when, as it should be, the wine is gently served.

Now to the question, when and with what kind of a meal we can or should drink Mosel or Rhine wines. When the weather is warm, it calls for either of them probably in preference to any other still wines. On cooler days, the more powerful wine, the Rhine wine, will be preferred to a Mosel. Both will suitably accompany any food which is not highly seasoned, or which of its own has such a dominating taste that it will not allow any other.

It is obvious that one can drink one kind of white wine all through a meal, but if the party is sufficiently large to allow it, a Mosel for the start, in particular with the fish, and a Rhine wine of some volume to follow with the roast or a similar dish will be successful. Always try and think of leading up; this, after all, is also the reason why you do not reverse meals; why you do not give the roast before the fish!

In fact, the art of serving wines is perfectly simple if you follow your natural inclination, your memory and your imagination. Take courage, and you will have a lot of fun and pass it on to others. It might, however, still be useful to add that sweet, powerful wines such as those of the highest class of Rhine wines are better not served throughout a meal. They will be better enjoyed when consumed after introduction by a lighter specimen.

A week on the Rhine and Mosel will acquaint you better with their wines than many words. You will then appreciate the praise so frequently given to the unique combination of wine, landscape and old civilization, all so different in the various districts. With a little more time you might even start in the very south with the Black Forest and Lake Constance, and enjoy the light and fragrant wines of Baden. You might then cross over from Heidelberg to the Palatinate, and notice at the foot of the Haardt Mountains how these protect the vast and rich area of vineyards, and you might enjoy some of their products in the middle and best part between Neustadt and Bad Dürkheim, along what is appropriately called the Weinstrasse. This road leads you north into Rheinhessen, begin-

ning at Worms with its Liebfrauenstift, from which the name
and fame of Liebfraumilch originated. At last you reach the
Rheingau and the most beautiful part of the Rhine. You will
be reminded of the close connexion between Church and
viticulture, which found tremendous expansion on the highest
level through monasteries during the Middle Ages, with
Schloss Johannisberg, formerly a Benedictine monastery, as a
striking example.

Leaving the Rhine at Coblenz, you arrive at the totally
different and much more intimate valley of the Mosel. The
common feature of both districts, the Rheingau and the Mosel,
is their delightful and at the same time so highly practical
background of the mountainous forests that shield the vineyards from rough winds and help to hold the warmth of the
sun in the valleys. The most famous Mosel names are halfway
down the river, names such as Trittenheim, Piesport, Brauneberg, Bernkastel, Zeltingen.

One should be warned against one rather common pitfall
of a holiday in a Wine District. One's frame of mind is such
that, on a wonderful summer's day with a raging thirst—
intensified perhaps by a good walk—these wines, nicely
cooled and very likely consumed in the open air, taste quite
perfect, even those inexpensive wines which are served by the
glass. These may, however, be wines which have not been
treated for bottle ripeness, and are delicious when quite
young. Enjoy all that on the spot but do not let enthusiasm
run away with you or expect such wines to taste the same
when you find them in your everyday mood detached from
the holiday atmosphere. It is exactly this which is at the bottom
of the story of wines which are said "not to travel." Indeed,
in this respect as with other questions of your purchases, it is
best to take the advice of a reliable wine merchant of your
own country. He must become your friend: you must be
able to trust him. Guided by real knowledge, and free of
prejudice, he might put you on to a vintage which is generally
not quoted as great, and he may be absolutely right in doing so.

There is nothing more difficult than to give a general' rule about great vintages. Even in great vintages some regions have failed; on the other hand, fine wines have been produced by vintages which generally gave only modest results. In the case of the famous 1921 vintage you will hear that some of the Palatinate growths got so much sun that the grapes were practically sunburnt, lacked the necessary acids, and produced wines far too concentrated, with too much alcohol. The very same vineyards in the rightly lower-classified 1920 vintage brought forth a number of the greatest *Spätlese* wines ever produced, infinitely better than their 1921s.

With this in mind, let us think for a moment of vintages of which some may still come our way: 1933 was a small crop, but produced excellent wines in individual districts, as good as or even better than the great vintage of 1934. I admire the 1934s, yet there were many Mosels and Rheingaus of the 1935 vintage which delighted us with most elegant wines of even more pronounced bouquet than those of its great forerunner. 1937 might be placed on as high a level as 1934, which was not reached again until 1945.

I doubt whether all 1947s will keep all their original promises; but quite a number of 1948s have got what 1947 sometimes lacks, the breed and distinction of a fine wine, and in this respect they frequently surpass the highly praised vintage of 1949—undoubtedly the greatest of the 1940s, though careful selection of its growths is necessary.

We know it is a thankless role to be cast as the successor of a great one: yet 1950 proved better than had been expected at the start. The 1953s, with their distinctive character and bouquet, were great wines; and although careful selection is necessary, 1959 was also a great year.

Many are the worries of the grower until the results of all his exertions are reaped. The wood must have survived the winter well; a quickly passing blossom is the next condition; then a summer with plenty of sun and not too little rain; and then an autumn without frost before the grapes have ripened, so that the gathering can be delayed, in order to obtain the *Spätlese* (later gathering), making possible too the *Auslese* (the selection of the best grapes). In a first-rate vintage, one may even separate from their own bunches those grapes which have reached a state of over-maturity and have them picked thus and vatted by themselves, a process giving the most exquisite of wines, the *Beeren-auslese*.

Such expressions are sometimes to be found on the label added to both the actual geographical region and the specific vineyard name. Thus, for example, Forst is the geographical place description, generally appearing adjectivally as "Forster," and followed by perhaps the word "Kirchenstück," the name of the vineyard; concluding, as may be apposite, with *Beeren-auslese*. There are numerous variations; you might, for instance, also find mentioned the name of the vine from which the wine was derived, e.g., Riesling.

How long a wine should be kept depends first of all upon the storing conditions; in a cool cellar a white wine will retain its qualities much longer than under other conditions. All the lighter types are ready a few months after bottling; some already mentioned will improve their bouquet and character greatly if stored for a couple of years; and only the finest qualities are worth keeping for many years. No definite time-limit can be set, for such a great deal depends on the composition of the vintage, for the success of which a harmonious combination of richness and acids, ensuring its keeping power, is essential.

In the German wine-districts it is usual for all finer wines to be kept separately after the gathering of the grapes, so that wines of identical description, from the very same vineyard and the same grower, may vary considerably and have a very different value. When you consider that more often than not these vineyards are owned by a number of proprietors, that the care and supervision of the vineyards may be different, and that the gathering of one proprietor may have been achieved under better weather conditions than that of his neighbour, you will readily understand also why prices differ.

Trinke nie als wär's zum Spiel
Der Weise schiesst nicht über's Ziel
Er trinkt bedächtig aber viel.

Wine is not a childish sport:
Go too far, its value's nought.
Drink a lot, but give it thought.

May this be the motto!

❧ ❧ ❧

IMPORTANT DISTRICTS AND VINEYARD PARISHES

Palatinate: Ruppertsberg, Deidesheim, Forst, Wachenheim, Dürkheim, Ungstein.

Franconia: Würzburg (Steinwein).

Rhenish Hessia: Worms (Liebfrauenstift), Oppenheim, Nierstein, Nackenheim, Bingen (Scharlachberg).

Rheingau: Rüdesheim, Geisenheim, Winkel (Schloss Vollrads), Johannisberg, Oestrich, Hattenheim (Kloster Eberbach: Steinberg), Hallgarten, Erbach (Marcobrunn), Kiedrich, Eltville, Rauenthal.

Mosel: Trittenheim, Neumagen, Dhron, Wintrich (Ohligsberg Geierslay), Piesport, Brauneberg, Bernkastel, Graach (Josefshof), Wehlen, Zeltingen, Uerzig, Erden, Traben-Trarbach, Enkirch.

Saar: Serrig, Ockfen, Ayl, Wiltingen (Scharzhofberg), Oberemmel (Scharzberg).

Ruwer: Kasel, Mertesdorf (Grünhaus), Eitelsbach (Karthäuserhof), Avelsbach.

❧ ❧ ❧

RECENT VINTAGES ON THE RHINE AND MOSEL

The following were renowned and outstanding
vintages, but many fine wines were made since
1934 in years other than those mentioned. Editor.

1949   1953   1955   1959   1961   1962   1964   1966   1967
1969   1972

V · WINES OF ALSACE

BY STANLEY F. DAVIS

THE merit of the wines of Alsace was little known and appreciated in Britain prior to the 1914-18 War. This was due largely to the fact that the territory was under German rule, and nearly all the wine was sold to Germany at the cheapest possible prices for blending purposes. It was not until the return of Alsace to France that wines of quality were made, as they had been prior to 1870; and soon there was a growing demand for them in many countries.

Unlike most viticultural regions of Europe, several different types of grape are used, producing a wide variety in the character of the various wines; some light and delicate and of a Moselle character, some heavier and sweeter—more like the Rheingau style. In fact, there is an Alsatian wine to suit every type of food and all purses—well filled or otherwise.

So far as English taste is concerned there are four main types, and they are named after the grapes from which they are made:

Sylvaner is of yellow-greenish colour, fresh, clean and appetizing. This wine develops quickly and has a short life. It is extremely attractive to drink as an *apéritif* or with a fish course.

Then comes the Riesling, producing firm, crisp, and very fresh wines, well balanced, and of great quality. In fact, the finest wines are always made from the grape of this name. In great years it is the King of the Vineyards. It has a golden colour, fine bouquet; it develops slowly and has the longest life.

The third wine is the Traminer, producing a softer, fuller-flavoured and more popular wine with a pronounced bouquet. It develops more quickly than the Riesling. It is in small production, and in many places is being replaced by the Gewürztraminer.

The Gewürztraminer produces a wine with a rich fruitiness and great aroma—very round and full flavoured, with a very pronounced bouquet. It keeps well and develops slowly, and can produce wines as luscious as a fine Sauternes but with a character all its own.

In addition to these four main types there are several wines which are not considered suitable for export: the full-flavoured and rather coarse Tockay; the somewhat similar Pinot Gris; the Pinot Blanc, which is a little like the Sylvaner; the Muscat d'Alsace, a dry wine with a full aroma; and there is a red Muscat as well. Both the Zwicker and Edelzwicker, or Gentil, are blended wines. You can drink these with pleasure in Alsace, and the Gentil is also very popular on the English market. It is neither too dry nor too sweet; it can be served equally well with bird or meat, and is a really useful wine to have where space does not allow of a varied cellar.

All Alsatian wines should be served too cold rather than too warm. They are at their best in the summer. If they are not really cold to start with, a warm room, warm glasses, and the length of time that passes before the glasses are emptied, may mean loss of much of their attraction.

The Alsatian vintner's life has not been an easy one: he has known many hardships and suffered much. Alsace has always been a buffer province over which Frank and Teuton have fought for hundreds of years; and under Louis XIV it was incorporated into the French Empire. In 1871, after the Franco-Prussian War, it was annexed by Germany, and 1918 saw it returned to France. In 1940, when France collapsed, it was again declared part of Germany, and it remained under German domination until the end of the war. Perhaps all these changes in rule, and the conditions under which the inhabitants have lived at various times, are greatly responsible for the wines of Alsace being generally known by the variety of grape from which they are made rather than by the actual place of production, for they have involved language and pronunciation difficulties, as well as changes of market.

The vintage commences during the last week in September, or, more often, the first week in October. Generally speaking, the more common grapes are the first to be gathered, i.e., those which are grown on ground running down to the river plain level. Then come the finer wines, such as the Traminer and Gewürztraminer, and finally the Riesling—which is always the latest in ripening. It is quite a common sight to see small proprietors pressing their grapes by the roadside in old-fashioned hand presses mounted on ox-carts! Fermentation commences almost immediately, and a long, slow fermentation is better for preserving the bouquet and character of the wine.

Generally speaking, the Sylvaner and the lesser Traminer wines are bottled in the spring following the vintage. The good Traminer, Riesling, Tockay and Gewürztraminer are left until the autumn; in fact, they can remain longer in cask if properly preserved, perhaps for two years or more.

Owing to the big difference in duty on foreign wines imported in bottle, as against those bottled in Britain, an increasing amount of Alsatian wine is being imported in cask. Generalizations are proverbially dangerous, but in the writer's opinion Alsatian wine, more especially the finer wines, are much better when bottled in Alsace, due probably to the technique which has been evolved over the years. This is a hint worth keeping in mind when choosing Alsace wines of the better quality.

The Alsatian countryside is well worth a visit. The scenery is beautiful, and the land is a gourmet's paradise. The German influence is most noticeable in the architecture of the villages, which are spotlessly clean, with no middens spilling over into the main street, as in so many French villages. The people are kind, cheerful, and extremely hospitable, and visitors can be assured of a delightfully friendly welcome. The variety of liqueurs you may obtain in the taverns is immense, with attractive names such as Framboises (made from wild fruits), Quetsch (from plums), Kirsch (from cherries), Myrtille, Sorbe, Mûre des Forêts and Prunelle Sauvage.

VI · WINES OF ITALY

BY FREDERICK ROSSI

MORE wine is made in Italy than in any other country in the world except France and it has great variety. Maybe this rich variety has something to do with the fact that the Italians have not made any concerted aim at achieving those qualities of refinement which mark the classified growths of the Médoc or the finer wines of Germany, but have been quite happy with the splendour of choice which one has among the wines of Italy—wines which have such notable liveliness and attraction, such richly sustaining qualities, such a high proportion of sugar and alcohol and such great fragrance and vinosity.

A glance at a map will explain one of the reasons for this variety in Italian wines. Right from the Swiss boundary in the north to Sicily in the south, in districts so different in so many ways, you will find vineyards where wine is made. The north

is the land of red wine; few good red wines are made far south
of the province of Tuscany. White wines are made from the
north to the south of the country. Nearly all, both red and
white, are beverage wines—to be taken with food, to quench
thirst. A notable exception, Italian Vermouth, is made in the
north-west with Turin as the main trade centre.

Let us consider Italy's red table wines. The main red wines
exported are: Chianti, Barolo, Barbaresco, Valtellina, Barbera, Capri, Lacrima Christi, Falerno, Orvieto.

There can be no doubt that Chianti is the most popular of
all. At least three centuries ago it was brought to Britain and
has never lost favour there. It has a lovely ruby colour and is
not too heavy in body, though it has no great refinement and
breed. It is an everyday wine, a wine that makes its appeal
straight away. Its bright liveliness gives it a special attraction,
and it has an average of 12 per cent of alcohol, with a good
balance of tannin and tartar, and it has a fair longevity if
given reasonable care.

In Tuscany there has been some disagreement about the
boundaries of Chianti country, and the Italian Government
has formed a committee to protect the fair name of the wine,
so that on every original flask you will now find a stamp carrying a number and the picture of a cockerel. Chianti is made by
a careful blending of different grapes, the Sangioveto to give
strength and character, the Trebbiano for colour and softness,
and the Malvasia for aroma and finesse. The making of this
wine has been for centuries the particular care of some of the
noble families of Tuscany, the Ricasolis and the Niccolinis
among others. Perhaps the Brolio Chianti is the best of all,
with the sound and dependable Chianti Ruffino among the
most popular.

How greatly is the attraction of this bright and lively wine
increased by the romantic Tuscan flask with its straw cover-
ing! You may buy Chianti in a half-litre, a litre, and double-
litre, and the small size is enough to provide three or four
quite generous glasses at a reasonable cost.

One of the most interesting things about Chianti is its method of fermentation. How ancient it is one can only guess. It is called the *governo*, a slow re-fermentation brought about in the body of the wine by the addition of "must" prepared from grapes picked a few days prior to the vintage and left to dry. The mould is cleaned from them, and they are allowed to ferment in a vat; this wine is racked of the pips and skins and then is added to the new wine in certain proportions, so starting a secondary fermentation. There is thus an increase in alcohol and a lowering of acidity. It is this which brings out the fragrance and vinosity and causes the liveliness—I can think of no better word—which one acclaims in every flask of good Chianti.

Very different is Barolo. Often described as the king of Italian table wines, it is big and full-bodied, with a deep-red colouring. This wine is grown on the ferruginous hillsides of Piedmont; it improves considerably with age, and amply repays the care which good growers bestow upon it. It largely owes its reputation to the assiduity of the Marquis of Barolo. After three or four years in wood the wine is bottled and laid down. It needs keeping in a cellar at constant temperature, and after six or seven years it throws a crust and loses some of its rich ruby colour, assuming a more tawny shade with a hint of old gold in its depths. Usually bottled in Burgundy bottles, Barolo is exported on a large scale, both to Britain and to North and South America.

Barbaresco is another aristocrat, grown also in Piedmont, on hills along the River Tanaro. It is not made on so large a scale as Barolo, and is a slightly lighter wine, softer and maturing more quickly. Its bouquet reminds one a little of violets.

Valtellina is grown in the most important district of Lombardy. As a rule, it is sold under individual names such as Sassela, Inferno and Grumello, and it is notable for its rich ruby colour and strong perfume. After a few years in bottle it develops a decided character of its own.

How different is Barbera from nearly all the wines I have

dealt with! It is big, heavy, generous. It makes no claim to
refinement. It is very popular in the north of Italy and is
exported to nearly every part of the world where there is an
Italian colony of any size. I think I would call it a wholesome
rustic wine, very dark red in colour, with an alcoholic content
that often reaches 14·5 per cent. Its tannin helps it to clarify
quickly in cask; and while it is slightly astringent and acid in
its earliest days, Barbera improves with age, the youthful
roughness softening somewhat. While it loses some of its
colour, it develops an attractive vinosity and vivacity. Unlike
some Italian wines, it travels excellently in most climates.
Much of the Barbera wine could be described as dry, but there
is a sweeter variety which the Italians describe as *amabile*,
containing a small percentage of unfermented sugar.

If the wines of Falerna have a great pedigree, and were
even praised by Horace, they are not so popular today as they
were in the ancient world. The white type is a medium dry
wine, amber in colour, high in alcohol. On the other hand, the
wine of Orvieto (in Tuscany) has become so popular in recent
years that it has outstripped the original area of production.
It has been said that its most attractive dumpy, straw-covered
flask has a good deal to do with this increase; but whatever
may be the truth in this there can be no doubt that Orvieto
is a most delightful golden-yellow wine, of good alcoholic
degree, and fairly sweet in flavour. I must add that there is
also a certain quantity of dry white Orvieto made, a wine that
goes well with fish and shell-fish.

Capri, the most famous island in the Mediterranean, has
its own wine. But it is an illusion to think that all the wine
sold as Capri is made on the island. Its total production could
not by any means satisfy the demand for this wine with so
romantic a name. And so growers of the white grapes on the
island of Ischia and in the Vesuvian districts around Naples
have been permitted to give the name Capri to the wine they
make, and of these the quality varies. The genuine Capri wine
is of a pretty, light-straw colour, with a fine bouquet, which

increases and improves with age. The taste is clean and completely dry, with no trace in it of unfermented sugar. I would recommend it as one of the most suitable of all Italian wines to accompany the fish course, and I would also stress that when it is chilled it is an excellent quencher of thirst on a hot day.

One cannot wonder, surely, that the popularity of Capri wine is increasing very quickly. The great number of tourists who visit this lovely island each year carry away with them such romantic impressions that, on their return home, they take pleasure in drinking Capri wine and recalling delightful memories. For those who are interested in the question of a wine's alcoholic strength, I would add that Capri averages about 11 per cent. The red wine, it must be said, is not nearly so popular as the white.

Lacrima Christi is a wine of great fame and antiquity. As with Capri, the red type is much the less popular. The wine is made from grapes grown in the volcanic districts around Vesuvius, and the best of all is made on the southern and eastern slopes of the Neapolitan hills from the white grape called Greco della Torre. This grape has a delightful light and fine aroma which is not lost in the unusually slow fermentation. The wine is low in sugar and tannin; and with an average of 12 per cent of alcohol it can fairly be described as a most pleasant dry, clean wine.

Many centuries ago, halfway up the slopes of Vesuvius, a hermit established himself with the intention of passing his life in prayer and penance. This saintly person, who took pleasure in helping and guiding passing travellers, thought it might be an excellent thing to set aside for sale some of the wine he had made, and one day a strange traveller paused and asked if he might stay at the lonely hermitage for a short time. He turned out to be none other than the Devil himself, and his design was to tempt the poor hermit to drink so much of his own wine that he would become drunk. The Prince of Evil had almost succeeded in his impious plan when a terrific storm of thunder and rain sent him scurrying off in terror, and so the hermit's soul was saved from perdition. Imagine the amazement of the holy man when he again tasted his rather poor and acid wine. He found it transformed into the most exquisite nectar! The transformation, he decided, could have been made by one thing only. At the moment when his soul was about to perish the tears of Christ had fallen ... and from that hour he decided to name his wine Lacrima Christi. Among the different legends about the wine of Vesuvius, I prefer this one.

Of Soave, from the Verona district, there is both a sweet and a dry variety. The alcoholic content of both is 12 per cent, and I am not surprised that both wines are becoming more popular every year both in Italy and in Britain.

A beautiful, limpid, golden wine is the Castelli Romani, which is grown in Frascati and other *communes* to the south of Rome. The yellow Trebbiano grape is used to produce a full, sweet, attractive wine, which is one of the most popular of all wines drunk by the discerning folk of Rome. Perhaps it ought to be noted that it has a fairly high alcoholic content, ranging up to 14 per cent.

I must also mention that golden muscatel wine, Est Est Est, with its odd name said to have been chalked on a tavern door to tell a bishop on a journey that the wine within was, most emphatically, good. Another fine product of the muscatel grape is Asti Spumante, one of the most famous sparkling wines in the world. Spumante means sparkling, and the wine is made on a system similar to that of Champagne, but it is much more luscious and fruity—and this probably explains its popularity with the ladies.

South, at the toe of Italy, lies the great island province of Sicily, where a considerable variety of wine is produced. Perhaps the best known of all is that of Marsala, a fortified wine which in some ways might be compared to certain Sherries. One of the richest of the muscatel wines is the Moscato of Syracuse; and at Palermo is the Zucco, also a pleasing dessert wine. In addition to these, Sicily produces a number of table wines, one of which is named Etna, and another is the Albanello, both sweet and dry, with a higher alcoholic percentage than the unwary might imagine.

There can be no doubt that the best place to drink Italian wine is in Italy. Who has not brought back memories of a seat upon a terrace under a vine, looking out to sea and watching the setting sun, and beside one a glass of wine which tastes all the more delicious because of the romantic scene? It must be admitted that many Italian wines do not travel well, but some take little harm from the journey by sea and rail, provided they are given time to rest in cellar or wine-cupboard before drinking. Among these are the following: Barolo, Barbera, Valtellina, Valpolicella, Cortese Bianco Secco, Orvieto, Chianti, Albana, Capri, Lacrima Christi, Est Est Est.

VII · A GATHERING OF MANY WINES

BY H. WARNER ALLEN

THE Norseman are said to have crossed the Atlantic before Columbus and found a New World with such a profusion of grapes that they named it Vineland, but in truth for nearly two millennia France has been the Vineland of the world. Remove the brightest stars of its vineyard constellation and there remains a list of lesser luminaries such as no other country can boast.

Taking its wine country as a whole, one can follow a continuous and gradual development of the character of its wines, arising from climate, soil and variety of vine, and trace, particularly in the case of red wines, the stages by which the fermented juice of the grape attains the qualities which give to each district its special renown. In the Midi the enormous production of ordinary wine which has its counterpart across the Mediterranean in Algeria makes no attempt to exploit the

higher possibilities of the vintage. Generally speaking the soil
is too rich, the sun too prodigal of its favours, to give the vine
a fair chance; it is only at its best when it has to struggle for
its life. Modern methods of vinification have improved these
wines without raising them above the level of an agreeable
beverage. Dessert wines such as Frontignan, Lunel, Rive-
saltes, to seduce the sweet tooth, are still to be found in this
region, though they have suffered much from the competition
of artificial substitutes.

The pattern of the great French wines may be said to start
with the Rhône, with the southernmost of its famous vineyards, Châteauneuf-du-Pape. Vines grown in a wilderness of
stones fight for their lives under a scorching sun; no less than
eleven varieties of grape are grown, each contributing its
quota to the tempered fire and extreme vinosity of the matured
wine. When young it is almost as fierce as the Vino dei Tempii
at Girgenti, in Sicily, and it is only when time has matured
its colour to the "onion-peel" hue that its violence is softened.
This is the characteristic of all the red Rhône wines, and I
always connect it with the granite which generally forms
the bedrock of the vineyard—granite plus great heat.

The finest of all *vins rosés* is to be found in this Avignon
neighbourhood at Tavel, on the right bank of the river. Its
amethyst colour makes it a wine apart, and its suavely delicious
aroma lacks the heat and fury of other Rhône wines, even
when it is quite young. It is fermented with skins, pips and
stalks like other *vins rosés*, until sugar and alcohol are about
evenly balanced, and then the foaming must, already rich in
colouring matter, is removed from the *marc* and fermented
apart as though it were a white wine.

The next great wine district lies some seventy miles farther
up the river at Tain with the vineyards of Hermitage, the most
celebrated of all the Rhône wines. "An ancient Hermitage,"
chirruped Meredith's Dr. Middleton, "has the light of the
antique; the merit that it can grow to an extreme old age."
One might add that like Châteauneuf-du-Pape it must be old

if it is to be drunk with pleasure; for all these wines fully fermented with the *marc* (the juice of stalks, pips and skins) need time to work out the crudity of their tannin. Hermitage occupies the highest rank in the Gotha of the Rhône wines, and it marks a step in advance of the wine grown farther south in the direction of Burgundy aristocracy. It cannot claim the breed and rare harmonies of the Côte d'Or wines, but it boasts a magnificent volume of flavour and body. The special Rhône grape, the Syrah, which has its share in Châteauneuf-du-Pape and about which many legends are told, flourishes on the hill above Tain in a thin layer of calcareous soil above the granite, the presence of chalk adding, as always, distinction and finesse to moderate the fierceness of the bedrock.

Farther north, south of Lyons, the wine of Ampuis, Côte Rôtie, marks a further approach to the dignity of Burgundy. It lacks the barbaric splendour of Hermitage, but it is a most agreeable wine, rich in bouquet and full-bodied. Here the important red Rhône wines come to an end. North of Lyons, Beaujolais and Mâconnais provide the transition to the Côte d'Or, where soil, climate and vine combine to produce a wine with the highest qualities of the Rhône wines, yet free of their tendency to excess.

The white wines of the river valley may be classified by that distinctive flavour to which the French give the name of *pierre à fusil,* gun-flint. Its development cannot be reduced to a geographical pattern, for it is prevalent in them all, strong in the white Châteauneuf-du-Pape, exaggerated in the more ordinary wines of the Côtes du Rhône, and at its best in white Hermitage, a very big wine with a most distinctive bouquet and flavour of its own.

Of a glorious golden colour, the quality of Hermitage is more akin to that of Montrachet than that of any other wine, though there is a certain coarseness in the intensity of its aroma which prevents it attaining the exquisite refinement and balance of the greatest white Burgundy. Its life exceeds that of the red Hermitage, and it will outlive even Dr. Middleton's ninety-year-old Port. Its gun-flint flavour is well blended in a general harmony of agreeable tastes. When I was a child I used to amuse myself by striking flints together to make sparks, and the smell of the stones warmed by the friction is reproduced in this special wine savour. It becomes a *terroir* tang in the coarser wines grown between Lyons and Givors.

To return to the gradual evolution of the red wines, the Rhône district is continued on the north by the Beaujolais and Mâconnais, which provide the transition to the Côte d'Or where the finest qualities of the Rhône wines are raised to a higher degree of artistic excellence. Burgundy has its own chapter, and before the trail of Bacchus is followed to his next avatar in vinous form a word must be said about a very curious wine grown in the Jura near Arbois.

Château Châlon is the only wine in the world which can claim an affinity to the wines grown far away in Spain and known to us as Sherry. It may be only a coincidence that this part of France was under Spanish rule until Louis XIV, but it is certain that it owes its special qualities to the same *flowering* process, or secondary fermentation, as the wine of Jerez. Like some Sherry, it is exceedingly dry, gains alcoholic strength as it ages, and is almost immortal.

The red-wine pattern carries us from the Côte d'Or to the great semicircle of the Loire, the longest river in France. Here it is easy to discern the transition stage between the splendour and dignity of Burgundy and the grace and feminine charm of Claret. Tours is the halfway house where the Burgundian Pinot grapes and the Cabernet of Bordeaux join hands, as the traveller will perceive if he makes a comparison between Chinon 1947 and Saint Avertin 1949 at the Fouqueux restaurant of Saint Avertin. The wines of the Breton grapes (as they call the Cabernet in Touraine) emphasize the flower scents and sweet fruit tastes of Claret, associated perhaps particularly with Margaux and often compared to the perfumes of violet and raspberry. They are as gay and sweetly smelling as a bed of wallflowers on a spring morning, and their chief shortcoming is a tendency to flabbiness when they are too soft and sweet.

The Chinon is wonderfully round and satiny, but is inclined to cloy, and it is interesting to see how this inclination was corrected in the Saint Avertin by the manly and sobering influence of the Pinot grapes. It must not be thought that flabbiness characterizes all the red Touraine wines. I think that the Bourgeuil wines are better made than the Chinon, and it is hard to imagine a more delightful wine on a hot day that a Bourgeuil of 1947, and another of 1943, which I tasted fresh from the cellar of their grower.

The white wines of the Loire, Vouvray in particular, are more famous than the red, though I think that they are inferior in quality. When unsophisticated, they are very refreshing country wines with a tendency to sparkle like Moselle, though they cannot rival the flower-like charm of the German wine, and their natural sprightliness has often tempted their growers to degrade them to the rank of imitation Champagne. *Communes* less known than Vouvray in Touraine, Montlouis for instance, are often truer to the tradition of trusting to nature; and in Anjou the Côteaux du Layon produce a rather sweet wine with a unique quince-like flavour which I much prefer to the produce labelled Saumur. Farther down the Loire ordinary white wine is made in the *pays du muscadet*.

Spain comes third in the list of European wine-growing countries. The wines of Jerez de la Frontera have since the days of Sack (which I believe not to be derived from *seco*, dry, but from *saca*, export, for the Sacks were sweet wines specially made for export) represented Spanish wines in England; but, as in Italy, there are a number of table wines quite pleasant to drink in their national home. There is Tarragona, once a Port substitute, and Beni-Carlo, almost as dark as the black wines of Cahors, which found its way into bottles with quite other labels—the best that can be said of them is that their abundance once helped to provide the French Army with war *pinard*, when Pétain doubled the wine ration.

Everywhere one drinks Rioja from Aragon, a wine usually of considerable body and alcoholic strength, but deficient in delicacy and finesse, though I once tasted an old Rioja Marqués de Riscal which really deserved to be hailed as great. Valdepenas is highly spoken of, but I cannot say that Malaga, the sweet wine made from the Pedro Ximenez grape, which under the name of Mountain was once more popular than the rich Sherry of the Victorian times, has any great appeal for me.

Portugal can claim some excellent table wines. I used to enjoy at Oporto the *vinho verde of* the Minho valley which, made from grapes grown high above the ground, possessed a singularly refreshing light acidity most delightful in hot weather. In those days the Douro *consumo,* the wine which fortification transforms into Port, was coarse and heavy, but now methods of vinification have been so improved that it has become an admirable beverage wine. The golden Bucellas, said to be grown from the same vine as the German Riesling, can be really good if it is free from the sulphur that is sometimes too obtrusive in it.

The first vineyard I ever saw, and the first wine I ever tasted in its native home, was in Switzerland. I still remember the impression of entering a new and exotic world produced upon my schoolboy mind by the ordered rows of vines running up the hillside behind our hotel at Montreux. Many years later, some forty years ago, I stayed at Chexbres above the Lake of Geneva with a friend from Bordeaux who had been making a methodical inspection of the Swiss vineyards. He was much struck by the excellence of the Swiss vines and grapes.

"I am not going to give these people any hints about wine-making," he remarked. "If they knew more about it, they might well be growing better wines than we do!"

The Swiss would scarcely claim today to be surpassing the better wines of France, but there has certainly been of late a quite remarkable improvement in the quality of their production. Of late I have tasted some really praiseworthy white wines of Neuchâtel, young, light and fresh, and full of the true grape flavour. André Simon introduced me to one as the herald of a fine Claret, and later a friend brought with him from Switzerland a bottle for my delectation. He was full of admiration for the care and skill with which the white Neuchâtel wines were made from the Fendant or Chasselas grape. Dézaley, from the Canton of Vaud, is sometimes ranked as the best of the Swiss wines, but I still uphold the premiership of my first love, Yvorne. Even if it is a trifle sweet on my adult palate, I can remember how I greeted with delight Morton Shand's reference to Yvorne in his *Book of Wine*: "For sheer delicacy of flavour, breed, and refinement of perfume, it would be hard to surpass these wines even among the classic Rheingau Hocks."

The Swiss red wines play second fiddle to the white, though the Dôle de Sion is a wine of real quality. Dôle is in this case the name of the grape and has no connexion with the town of Dôle in the French Jura. Mr. Shand speaks of a red Neuchâtel wine, Cortaillod, as possessing the characteristics of a fine Mercurey with greater fire and body. The finest Swiss wines are grown in the cantons of Vaud, Valais and Neuchâtel.

Many local wines do not travel well and can be drunk to full advantage only in or near the countryside where they were grown. They provide entrancing adventures for the traveller, who may return home with news of discoveries that cannot, alas, be shared with those who do not themselves go out upon the road of romance into the vinelands. But quite a surprising variety of wines from different countries and regions can be bought in Britain, and shipments large or small come from Algeria, Chile, Corsica, Cyprus, Greece, Hungary, Luxembourg, Palestine, Turkey, Yugoslavia. When you are in a mood to try experiments, let your wine merchant be your guide.

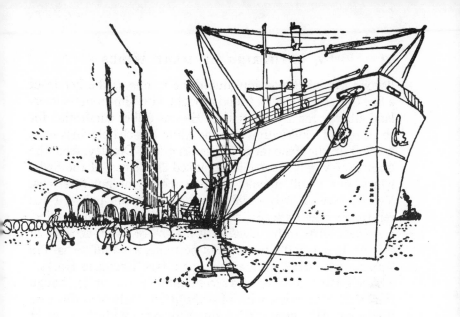

VIII · SOUTH AFRICAN AND AUSTRALIAN WINES

BY JOHN BURGOYNE

A CURIOUS failing many Britishers suffer from is that of believing that something imported and foreign *must* be better than a similar British or Commonwealth article. In painting, music and the arts generally—in Paris hats most notably—how often do we see the second-rate extolled because of its foreign origin in preference to the finer, which happens to be British. But, it may be argued, Paris *does* produce the finest women's hats in the world, however second- or third-rate some may be. This is a subject on which, as a mere male, I should hate to dogmatize. I will readily concede the argument, nevertheless, as it supports my contentions about wine.

If some wellwisher were to offer me the dinner that would give me the greatest pleasure, aesthetic and otherwise, I would without hesitation select to go with it one or more of the great

French Clarets. I am fortunate enough, through my upbring-
ing, to be able to appreciate some of these great wines and,
without any fear of contradiction, say that no country in the
world can produce natural red wines comparable with the
finest growths of the Bordeaux area of France. The difficulty
is that these wines are normally beyond the means of most
people in this tough modern world, and the pleasures they can
give have to be confined to rare occasions. There, in one sentence, lies the gist of what I wish to convey.

To get down to brass tacks, what the great majority of wine-
drinkers want—and can afford—for daily drinking is sound,
honest, well-made wine, with reasonable maturity, at the
lowest cost per bottle.

It is at this stage that the difficulties begin to rear their
heads. A quart of so-and-so oil for the car, a bottle of such-
and-such sauce, are, one can assume, products that can be
bought with every confidence; they are standardized articles.
But wine refuses to be standardized. It is living, and it changes
from month to month and year to year. We must learn to
exercise judgment, to appreciate the contents of the bottle,
rather than just "to drink the label." We must realize that,
although certain countries in the old continent of Europe
produce wines that are unrivalled throughout the world, some
of their lesser and cheaper wines seem to be sheltering under
the reputation of the finest growths of the country concerned
—and in my opinion certainly not all of them give the best
value in a wine for ordinary drinking at prices that range from
the lowest grade to a figure approaching £1 a bottle.

The two great countries of Australia and South Africa fall
into a category of their own. They are both young, virile
nations. Australia planted her first vineyards about a century
and three-quarters ago, while the year 1952 marked the tercen-
tenary of wine-making in the Cape. That is a very short time
in the history of wine and, in certain aspects, the two countries
are still feeling their way. As yet neither of them produces in
marketable quantities those very exceptional and necessarily

high-priced wines that stand on a pinnacle of their own. They
have the climate, the soils and the enthusiasm—and who
knows what truly great wines they may yet make! But, as I
have said, most of us are searching for *value* in return for our
hard-earned cash, and it is here that the wines of which I
speak come into their own, for the general standard of quality
is high.

That is a bold statement, and I should like to give my
reasons for making it. The comparatively young industries in
Australia and South Africa are guided by fresh minds. They
have introduced modern methods of hygiene and cleanliness,
and are using the latest developments of science in their efforts
to guide Nature's processes in the right direction. In a word,
they use the microscope instead of guesswork.

One hears occasionally the somewhat disdainful comment
that Australian or South African wines are not worth drinking
—for "who wants his wine made in a factory?" As is usual,
there is an element of truth in this, if large-scale and utterly
clean modern wineries can be called factories. Suppose a
similar comment were made over your loaf of bread—that it
was inferior because the wheat had been harvested with a
diesel-engined combine harvester instead of with the traditional scythe? It is not that Nature's processes are being
disturbed, but simply that her products are being handled by
modern, economic methods.

What, then, are the types of wine that reach us from these
countries—and how is one to describe a wine so as to make
its general classification quite plain? The purists maintain
that the words "Australian Burgundy" or "South African
Sherry" are contradictions in terms. The average man, on the
other hand, prefers to regard these and other terms as being
the only ones in the English language that convey a general
description of the *sort* of wine he has in mind. I have myself
seen a catalogue printed over one hundred and seventy-five
years ago which listed "Spanish Sauternes" and "Spanish
Burgundy." To refer to a cow born in our own parish as a

HCW—D

"Jersey" cow engenders no heated argument! My own view is that as all these wines become more and more established on the British market their local names will gradually come into favour with the public, and the present method of description become less and less necessary.

Both Australia and South Africa make red and white natural wines and have a range of fortified wines of heavier alcoholic content of the Port and Sherry type. The light, white table wines of both countries have many admirers in Britain. As a rule, they are distinctly more "dry" than their European counterparts. This comparative lack of sweetness is directly due to the difficulty of shipping delicate, sugary white wines halfway round the world and across the equator. But wines such as Riesling or Traminer travel exceedingly well and are worth finding. They usually come from the cooler areas, such as the Hunter River district of New South Wales, near the sea, or from round Tulbagh in the Cape Province, which is a village in the mountainous highlands where cool breezes counteract the constant South African sunshine.

The "Burgundies" of Australia made a reputation for themselves in Britain nearly a century ago. They have been appreciated ever since. In general, they are extremely well-made wines, very robust, and reasonable in price. There is no doubt that wine of this style is invaluable to many convalescents and to those whose condition can be described as "run-down." These wines develop fairly quickly; an Australian Burgundy which has been in bottle for, say, ten years is further advanced than its European counterpart which has been bottled for twice that period. The South African Burgundy is usually a wine of lighter character and appeals more to those whose ideas have been moulded on European vintages.

As regards the lighter red wines, both countries have, in recent years, been producing fairly delicate wines, and I believe these "Clarets" will prove to be great favourites in the years ahead.

The light red and white wines of either country should not

be compared directly with the better-known wines of Europe. No one with experience of French wines would dream of comparing the Graves and Sauternes grown in the Gironde with the white wines produced a few hundred miles to the north, near the mouth of the Loire. As well compare the merits of two cheeses such as Gruyère and Camembert—which have equal, perhaps, but completely different qualities.

Even a cursory glance at the annual Customs returns would show the popularity of South African Sherries in Britain. Apart from their intrinsic merits, South Africa was fortunate, when the last war burst upon us, in having large, well-matured stocks ready for shipment. She came into her own during those trying years when Britain was largely cut off from the continent of Europe. The quality of her wines created a lasting reputation and fashion. Australia also is making some first-rate wines, which, in the opinion of some experts, can be superior even to the Cape Sherries; but, owing to Australia's buoyant home market, where they are consuming three or four times as much wine as they did in 1939, her finest wines are harder to find overseas. I do assure you they are worth searching for! Pass your wine merchant a hint and wait for him to produce a bottle for you to try.

Before the Second World War Britain consumed "Empire" wines in as great quantities as she did those of any European country. The wines shipped today are on the whole superior in quality to those of the inter-war years, well matured, soft and round, and in many instances very well worthy of a student's attention. If the import duties were lowered, giving adequate preference to a welcome product, which has to be brought halfway round the world, it follows that these wines would cost less and there would be a wider variety.

Nearly all of the lighter wines for ordinary use will keep for several days after the cork has been drawn, and the flagoned wines will keep longer still. Both the Port and Sherry types have great staying power after contact has been made with the air—a point worth noting for those who may wish for any reason to put a wine aside for several weeks after a bottle has been broached.

I am often asked what characteristics of a South African wine can be said to distinguish it clearly from an Australian. This is one of those questions to which there is, at present, no answer. All countries produce a wide range of wines, and I have known French experts to be hopelessly confused. They have judged a Cape Burgundy to be an excellent example of Rhône wine, and a full French wine—just because I had Australian connexions—to be a red table-wine from the Antipodes! Where great judges can be so puzzled, how can the ordinary consumer be expected to judge? The answer would seem to be: "I will try to ignore the country of origin on the label of this bottle of wine. I will judge the wine itself on its own merits." This is a simple request and is, at the same time, very hard to carry out. The influence of the name on the label is so very persuasive!

There are, however, some things that can be said about a number of these good wines. Note the freshness of flavour in many of the lighter white wines of South Africa; note the taste of the grape singing out so pleasantly in the Hock types. And you will find a happy absence of that whiff of sulphur which can be detected in some of the commoner white wines of Europe. All of these should, of course, be chilled before drinking.

In the wines of Burgundy type, note the fullness and robustness of the flavour; in these—the Australian wines especially—you have an alcoholic content that is equalled by few European wines of comparable quality, except good Italian wines and the heavier wines of the Rhône valley. And note how their fleshy "body" is modified and given an attractive balance by a little touch of dryness on the palate. This hint of astringency keeps the wine from having too great a fullness, gives it a certain balance. In wines of the Claret type, particularly those of South Africa, note the quick appeal they make to the palate; note how they bring out the flavour of the food which they accompany—one of their chief charms. It would be foolish to compare them to a fine Château Lafite of a good year. They have not the subtlety of bouquet, the overtones and undertones in their appeal to the palate, they have not yet gained all the suavity and "breed" which give the highest pleasure to a fully cultivated taste. But they are developing qualities of their own, and the day will come when they will have characteristics as clearly defined as those that mark off a Sauternes like Château d'Yquem from a great Hock like a Kallstadter Steinacker. And meantime, while they improve every year by the care and enterprise of workers of these distant vineyards, let us enjoy the wines for the qualities they can give us—and give us in so full a measure.

IX · SHERRY

BY CHARLES WILLIAMS

THE greatest variety to be found in one single wine is to be found in Sherry. Its colour ranges by infinite stages from that of pale straw, through graduations of gold and amber, to a rich, dark mahogany brown. On the palate it may be "bone" dry, extremely sweet, or anything in between. Its bouquet, or "nose" as the experts call it, is subtle and of an astonishing range. To appreciate Sherry is to be well on the way to appreciate all wines.

It follows that Sherry may be drunk before, at, or after a meal, or indeed without bothering about a meal at all. George Saintsbury, who wrote a characteristic sentence about the *adaptableness* of Sherry, once devised a "Sherry dinner" during which no wine except Sherry was to be served but every course was to be accompanied by an appropriate Sherry. To adapt some words of Dr. Johnson on another topic: "when a man is tired of Sherry, he is tired of wine; for there is in Sherry all (or pretty nearly all) that wine can afford."

Sherry has other virtues. It travels extremely well all over the world, and particularly to Britain, provided always that it has been shipped, as is the habit of all good shippers, at adequately high strength. In a decanter, or once the bottle has been opened, Sherry keeps in good condition longer than any other wine. Furthermore, there is no reason why one should not smoke while drinking Sherry, for tobacco does not seem adversely to affect either its aroma or its taste. In fact, one of the very best tasters of the Sherry trade in Spain used to smell and taste long lines of samples with a lighted pungent Spanish cigarette for ever in and out of his mouth.

Old Sherry, too, has considerable restorative properties, and in many households, rich and poor, in the south of Spain, any sudden illness is the signal to get out the bottle of old Pedro Ximenez, in the good offices of which every member of the family has a not unjustified faith.

Indeed, it is difficult to exaggerate the pleasure and interest that can be derived from trying and comparing different Sherries, and this taste can fortunately be indulged in Great Britain better and more easily than anywhere, because the British not only drink more Sherry, but better Sherry than any other nation, not excluding Spain herself. No doubt, after some experience, everyone will lean to one or two particular favourites, but in restaurants and bars and friends' houses one is always meeting unfamiliar Sherries, and it is fascinating to compare them. There is still a lot to be said for the final words of Falstaff's eulogy of the Sherry of Shakespeare's day, namely, Sherris-sack: "If I had a thousand sons, the first human principle I would teach them should be to forswear thin potations, and to addict themselves to Sack."

It is time, however, to define Sherry. It is a blended and fortified still wine made in South-west Spain, in or near Jerez de la Frontera, from the juice of white grapes grown in the surrounding country. Other wines made and grown elsewhere in the world make use of the name Sherry: but they are imitations of the original wine. They are sometimes made, it is true, from similar vine plants; but because they are always grown in different soils and climates they are far from identical with the original. This is recognized by the law of England, under which any wine labelled just "Sherry" has to be from the delimited area near Jerez, and any other wine calling itself Sherry has to be labelled, for example, "South African Sherry," "Cyprus Sherry," etc., with the name of the country from which it originates in as large letters as the word "Sherry" itself. This is to prevent purchasers being misled. Nevertheless, it is best to look always for the words "Produce of Spain" or their equivalent on the label.

Because Sherry is always a blend of wines grown in different vineyards in different years, no one need bother his or her memory with dates. There is no such thing as, for example, "1927 Sherry," or "Sherry, Vintage 1870"; and this, in a more and more complex world, is a great convenience to the amateur.

More than any other wine, Sherry depends on the skill and integrity of the shipper. For it is he who, year after year, has to make up in Spain sound palatable blends from his stock of very diverse wines, and preserve a steady continuity of colour, taste and bouquet in each such blend.

The best advice that can be given to a young man or woman who is beginning to drink Sherry is to acquire, first by repute and later by personal experience, a knowledge of the names of the best shippers, and then stick to the Sherries produced by them.

That Sherry is a fortified wine means in practice that all Sherry exported has, at various stages, had Grape-brandy added to bring it up to the usual level of 20 to 21 per cent alcohol by volume. This fortification preserves the wine during its maturing and transit through different climates and temperatures and ensures that it has sufficient "kick" to make it satisfying. For there is nothing, in temperate and cold climates, more mawkish than weak, wishy-washy Sherry. One hesitates in these days ever to suggest further legislation, but it might not be a bad thing if, as in the U.S.A., every bottle of Sherry had to carry a note of its strength plainly printed on the label.

The old town of Jerez de la Frontera in Andalusia, where true Sherry is made, is about the size of York and lies about twenty-five miles north-east of Cadiz (the port from which all Sherry is shipped), although it is itself only about fifteen miles from the Atlantic. It has many church towers and the remains of an old wall, and it is set in open country among small un-dulating slopes upon which are the vineyards, mainly owned and cultivated in the old-fashioned way by small proprietors, who sell their produce to the shippers. There are three types of soil: one (the best and rarest) white and chalky; another very dark; and the third sandy. These varieties of soil contri-bute to the variety of the wine. Rain, and plenty of it, in March is best for the vines, and then, beginning in May, the sun becomes hotter and hotter, while the grapes ripen and fill out with sweet juice ready for the vintage in early or mid-September.

Sherry grapes are gathered and pressed in the farmhouses near the vineyards in large, square, wooden troughs, called *lagares*. The pressing is done by country folk wearing special boots into the soles of which many small nails have been driven sideways. The object of this is that the pips and stalks shall be caught between the heads of the nails and thus not be crushed; if this happened the result would be an astringent wine with an excess of tannin.

As soon as the pressing is finished the juice, or, as it is then called, the must, is run off into new casks. For, just as the Bible tells us to put new wine into new bottles, so new Sherry ought to be put into new casks. The moment the grapes are pressed the must begins to ferment in the *lagar* and continues to fer-ment in the cask. As it is carried away, in bullock carts or lorries, from the vineyard to the shippers' premises it seethes, and froth pours out through the bunghole of the cask. It usually takes just under three weeks to complete its fermenta-tion, and all the time the casks are left out in the open air with the bung off.

Now comes something quite peculiar to Sherry. In a good year most of the wine, as soon as fermentation has ended, will begin to grow what is known as *flor*. This is a white organic growth which looks like little straggling shreds of cream-cheese lying on top of the wine.

The presence of this *flor* in large quantities in his new wine is extremely welcome to a Sherry shipper. The reason is this: There are two main types of Sherry—"Fino" and "Oloroso." Fino Sherry is very pale in colour and very delicate to the taste, and is permitted to develop more or less naturally for a number of years, growing *flor* all the while.

Oloroso Sherry, on the other hand, is Sherry which has never developed *flor* at all, or in which the growth of *flor* has been artificially stopped—as it always can be—by the addition of extra Grape-brandy. If it is desired that the wine should remain Fino and therefore continue to grow *flor*, only a limited quantity of Brandy per cask is put in. For Oloroso a larger quantity is put in and the wine has a darker colour, more body and, in its early life, a higher strength than Fino.

A shipper's premises in Jerez are known as his *bodega*. This consists of the firm's offices, the cooperage, and a number of very large, high-roofed warehouses, whitewashed inside and out, with big wooden doors, in which are ranged storage casks, partly, but never wholly, filled with Sherry, in three or four tiers. All Sherry is matured above ground in these large warehouses with the doors kept open all day long, the warm air circulating through, and the casks not bunged down tight, but each with a very lightly-fitting stopper just to keep the dust out. The result is that in a wine's two or three years in a Jerez *bodega* the evaporation is phenomenal, but that is the way Sherry matures and improves.

There is another stage in the production and maturing of Sherry which is quite special to Jerez: that is the famous *Solera* System, by means of which blends are made up and their continuity assured. This is an ancient method by which old Sherry wines and slightly younger Sherry wines are stored together in the same set of casks, so that the virtues of the older wines are communicated to the younger. This object is attained by drawing off, for blending, only small quantities of older wines from each cask in the set and then substituting for the wine drawn off a slightly younger wine of similar style and origin from another set of storage casks.

For example, suppose that a shipper has as an ingredient in one of his standard blends of Sherry a certain quantity from his Velasquez *solera*. (For easy reference each set of casks is given a name.) This Velasquez *solera* will consist of a set of, say, twenty storage casks, lying in his *bodega*, which are never moved and never racked. In making up some of that blend for shipment he does not draw all the Velasquez wine he requires off the same cask. On the contrary, he draws off from each cask an equal proportion of the total quantity required. In the instance given, if he requires for his blend, say, sixty gallons from the Velasquez *solera*, he will draw off three gallons from each of the twenty casks.

The Velasquez, however, is the oldest of a whole set of graduated *solera* leading up to it. Therefore the three gallons taken from each Velasquez cask are, as soon as convenient, replaced with wine drawn from the next *solera* in the scale—say, the Murillo *solera* of thirty casks. Once again an equal quantity of wine is drawn off each of the thirty Murillo casks and moved into the Velasquez ones; this quantity will obviously be two gallons from each cask. The process continues in exactly the same way in respect of a number of supporting *soleras*, each containing rather younger wine than does its predecessor.

At the end of the series it is necessary to put some wine into the youngest *solera*. Where does this wine come from? The answer is that it is two- or three-year-old wine which has never yet been in a *solera* and which has been maturing separately in the shipper's *bodega* ever since it was vintaged.

The reader will now appreciate that each time that any wine is required for a blend from a *solera* (and wine for shipment is always drawn off the oldest *solera* in a series) there is a progressive drawing off and filling up along the scale from one *solera* in the series to the next.

The matter does not end there. The blend in question probably calls, as part of its ingredients, for some quantity of wine from each of two or three other different *soleras;* and, since each of these will be backed by a set of younger *soleras,* the same process of drawing off from and filling up each will have to be undertaken.

The *Solera* System not only attains its object of marrying younger with older wine, it does something else as well. It ensures continuity of shippers' blends and of their ingredients —a continuity of style, quality and age. For naturally one vintage varies a good deal from another, and sometimes a whole run of good years or poor years may occur consecutively. If it were not for the *Solera* System, each shipment of a particular Sherry would vary and the public would cease to be able to rely, as they can now, on their favourite Sherries having the same body, bouquet and flavour year after year.

This description of the *Solera* System shows how impossible it is to put a date to any Sherry except to the two- or three-year-old Sherry that is kept separately. Most of the *soleras* in Jerez were started many years ago. In the casks containing the oldest wine in a series of *soleras* there will perhaps be a few drops of Sherry made in the 'eighties, some wineglassfuls of wine made in the 'nineties, some pints of wine of the early nineteen-hundreds, and so on and so on. In addition, two kinds of Sherry, made specially for blending, *Vino dulce* and *Vino de color,* are used in very small quantities for sweetening or touching up the colour.

It will be best to describe one by one the various Sherries available in Britain.

FINO   This should be a pale, delicate Sherry with a light, subtle bouquet, usually dry, and sometimes very dry, on the palate. It should be drunk before meals, or perhaps with the first course of a meal, especially if that course is oysters, hors-d'oeuvre, smoked salmon or something like that.

MONTILLA   This is a rare Fino wine, which is grown on a patch of best-quality white soil lying some distance from the Jerez vineyards, near the small town of Montilla, in the hills not far from Cordova. The production is small and consequently Montilla is never cheap. It is very pale and very, very dry. Indeed, one firm of shippers, borrowing a word usually applied only to Champagne, describe a Montilla wine of theirs as *brut* in order to emphasize its extra dryness as compared with the usual run of dry Sherries.

AMONTILLADO   This may be described as high-quality Jerez Fino wine grown on the best white soil and therefore, if it is genuine, never cheap. The name has an historical derivation. Towards the end of the eighteenth century Montilla wine became very much admired in Jerez, and the Jerez shippers set out to try to make a Fino Sherry in Jerez as near as possible in the style of Montilla wine. And, when they had made a wine as like Montilla as they could —though it was not really very close to Montilla— they called it Amontillado, meaning wine made like Montilla, and thus embedded the name Montilla in the middle of their new word.

VINO DE PASTO   Vino de Pasto is an unpretentious Fino wine, often not particularly dry. The words mean literally "wine of the repast."

MANZANILLA   This, like Chablis and Liebfraumilch, has been a much-abused name. Genuine Manzanilla is rare. It is high-quality, dry Fino wine with a peculiar tang. This tang is quite indescribable in words, but is unmistakable to anyone who has tasted the real article. The thing that makes Manzanilla different from other Fino Sherries is that it has to be made and matured close to the sea. There is something about the sea air during fermentation and maturation that does the trick. It is made and stored at a seaside place called Sanlucar de Barrameda, a little way to the north-west of Cadiz. Manzanilla means in Spanish the camomile flower, but no one has ever explained how the word came to be applied to the wine, which does not in the least taste like camomile. Confusion is apt to arise, however, in other parts of Spain, and there is a sad story of an Englishman who once motored through the north of Spain, murmuring the word "Manzanilla" at one café after another in the hope of being served with the wine, but always being fobbed off with camomile tea!

OLOROSO   Oloroso can be dry or sweet, but in Britain is more usually sweet than dry. Like Fino it may be drunk before meals, and, if the first course of a meal is soup, Oloroso goes very well with it. It is a particularly pleasant wine to drink with a biscuit or a slice of cake in mid-morning or at some other between-meals time. The heavier varieties are best drunk at the end of a meal.

AMOROSO   This is not a term used in Spain, but is a kind of bastard Anglo-Spanish way of describing a rather full, sweet or sweetish Oloroso. The word Amoroso is indeed a Spanish word and, defined as it is in the dictionaries as meaning "loving, affectionate, gentle," is not exactly an illuminating name for a type of Sherry.

GOLDEN SHERRY   This is a straightforward English term which means exactly what it says. The wine should be Oloroso of light or medium golden colour (as opposed to the light straw colour of most Finos), full-bodied, and rather sweet.

SOLERA SHERRY   This is a misnomer, perpetrated by the
English. From the account given above of the *Solera*
System it will be clear, first, that all Sherries are to
a large extent drawn from *soleras,* and, secondly,
that no Sherry-shipper, unless he were qualifying
for a lunatic asylum, would ever ship away whole
casks from any single one of his *soleras,* which are
his priceless stock-in-trade on which the future of
his business depends. Nor indeed would wine
shipped from a particular *solera* and unblended
with other·wines be at all palatable for ordinary
drinking. Solera Sherry is, in fact, an English fancy
name for a heavy, dark Oloroso, usually rather on
the sweet side.

BROWN SHERRY   Brown Sherry is unknown to the
Spanish consumer. It was created over a century
or more ago for the English market, from which the
taste for it has spread to other countries. It is very
dark brown in colour, sweet and luscious, and was
originally designed to be drunk after a meal alone
or in season accompanied by nuts. Nowadays it is
drunk by many people at all times of the day and
whenever they feel like it.

It may seem strange, in view of the rich, dark mahogany
hue of Brown Sherry, that it can have been made from white
grapes. The explanation is that the best Brown Sherry is made
from a special vine, the Pedro Jimenez vine, and that the
custom is for the grapes from this vine, as soon as they are
picked, to be laid in the sun on esparto-grass mats until they
begin to resemble raisins. They are then pressed and, as a
result, very little juice is obtained, but that juice is very dark,
very sweet and highly concentrated. It is for this reason that
really good Brown Sherry can never be cheap. It can also be
made by blending dark Oloroso, sweet wine and *vino de color,*
and the result is far from unpalatable, but never up to the

quality of Brown Sherry that has been made from Pedro Jimenez grapes which were vintaged in the manner I have described.

The best way to enjoy Sherry, and at the same time to inform oneself about it, is to begin by throwing away all snobbish ideas. As explained, Sherry is fortunately unaffected by the snobbery which attaches to dates and vintages. There is, however, another kind of snobbery, to which some Sherry-drinkers are prone and for which there is no real basis at all. This is the cult of "dry" Sherry. Very often this is not even a cult, but a pure affectation, which takes the form of asking for "dry" Sherry and wanting the adjective "dry" on the label, although in fact a *really dry* Sherry is the last thing that would be welcome.

How this particular piece of nonsense originated it is difficult to say. It probably came about because in the Sherry district itself, where the climate is entirely different from that of Great Britain, the Sherry served is usually dry. Be that as it may, genuine Sherry from Spain may be anything from very pale and very dry to very dark and very sweet, and surely it goes without saying that anyone is at liberty to drink whichever kind he likes and still know that he is drinking the real wine.

The best advice I can give to interested Sherry-drinkers is to experiment with various types and brands. Begin with the ordinary kinds of Sherry, perhaps Vino de Pasto as a Fino and Golden for an Oloroso.

Never lose an opportunity of tasting a new Sherry, and taste and smell and examine the first glass very carefully so that its impression on your eye, on your sense of smell and on your palate is recorded firmly in your mind. For it is necessary to bring all three senses into play at the same time. Remember the old Latin tag: *"Vina probantur odore sapore colore."* Do not let slip, even in earlier days, the chance of tasting one of the more unusual wines such as Montilla or Manzanilla, but do not seek after them till you are more experienced, and then do not be surprised or put out if, to begin with and even later on, you do not like them.

The drinking of wine should be a pleasure, not a duty, and the moment it becomes anything but a pleasure it is nothing but a boring foppery.

SHERRY SHIPPERS

There are about forty firms that ship Sherry to Britain, and the following are among the best known. Editor.

Diez Hermanos
Domecq, Pedro
Duff Gordon and Co.
Fernandez (Manuel) and Co.
Findlater, Mackie, Todd
Garvey
Gonzalez, Byass and Co.

Martinez, Gassiot and Co.
Misa, Manuel
De la Riva (M. Antonio) and Co.
Sandeman Bros. and Co.
Valdespino y Hermano
Williams and Humbert
Wisdom and Warter

X · PORT WINE

BY FREDERICK A. COCKBURN

"Port! Port! No Briton ought
Consider that he's done his Duty
Until he's felt beneath his belt
A bottle of the Rare Old Fruity."

THESE words, written by the late H. G. Pelissier, seem
to sum up the fact that Port has been the national drink
over a great number of years in England where it has
for long been the wine in which the Sovereign's health is
drunk. It was in 1353 that Edward III made a treaty with
Portugal which enabled Portuguese fishermen to fish for cod
off the coast of England, and during these trips they brought
over wine in skins and small casks which they bartered for
other goods. This was undoubtedly the first introduction of
Portuguese wine to the British Isles. One of the many reasons
why it has remained so popular is that it suits the climate so
admirably.

The original name of Port was *Vinho do Porto,* which
when translated means the Wine of Porto. In Portuguese *Porto*
means *harbour,* while the letter *O* means *the.* Even today the

Portuguese name of that great city is not Oporto but Porto, and so we find this particular Portuguese wine being denominated as "Porto Wine" or for short "Port Wine." Attempts are frequently being made to establish that the classic names of Port and Sherry are today no more than merely generic, but the only sound nomenclature for identifying a wine is that of its geographical district.

The Portuguese have by law marked out an area round the banks of the upper part of the River Douro. It is known as "the Douro district," and is the only part of the world whose wine can be sold under the name of Port.

This country is extremely hilly and the river winds its way through magnificent canyons. The scenery is wild and rugged, and clinging to the sides of the hills are vines growing in terraces built to prevent heavy rain from washing the soil away.

A great deal of wine is still brought down the river by the curious local boats, which have one sail and are steered from the stern by a long rudder. One's first impression of the Douro is one of almost eerie stillness, broken only by the occasional whistle of a train or the squeaking of the wheels of the bullock carts used for transporting the casks down the narrow paths through the hills.

The vineyards, known as *quintas,* are for the most part owned by farmers who make their wine for a shipper or sell him their *mosto*—the fermented juice without the addition of Brandy—and the wine is then made under the care of the shipper himself. The actual grape is much smaller than the ordinary hothouse variety used for dessert. Vintage takes place from the third week in September to the first or second week in October, depending on weather conditions and the state of the grapes.

The gathered grapes are carried to a building in long baskets and emptied into a large stone trough called a *lagar.* When the *lagar* is full, in order to start the fermentation, men enter it and march up and down, treading the grapes. Whilst more modern methods are sometimes used in various *quintas*, it is found that the old methods are really the best. When treading the wine the warmth of the human foot goes far to cause an even fermentation and gets the best out of the grape. Also, the pips and stalks are not broken, and thus released to spoil the wine.

According to the temperature and the time of treading, the juice starts to ferment. On the wine reaching the required degree of sweetness it is run off into large wooden vats called *tonels*, where, by the addition of a small quantity of Portuguese Wine-brandy, the fermentation is stopped. It is here that the skill of the shipper or farmer plays an important part, for his experience tells him what sort of wine is best made from any particular *quinta*. The longer a wine is allowed to ferment the drier it becomes: and if the fermentation, on the other hand, is stopped at a very early juncture, the result is a much sweeter wine, since the sugars have been retained. The *tonels* are thoroughly "roused" after the Brandy has been added, and the wines are then allowed to settle down through the cool winter months.

In the spring the wines are again fed with a little Brandy and are taken off their deposits (the lees) and transferred to single casks, known as pipes, which contain approximately one hundred and twenty gallons. The wine is then brought down to be stored in the shippers' lodges (warehouses) at Vila Nova de Gaia, which lies on the opposite side of the River Douro from Oporto.

When the wines are quite young they naturally have a full deep colour, but after a certain time in cask they lose colour and become ruby. The longer one keeps them in cask the lighter they become, passing from the full dark wine of their youth to Ruby, then to light Ruby, eventually to medium Tawny, Tawny, and finally light Tawny. In all these styles the features of dryness and sweetness can be supplied according to one's taste.

It would be as well to remember that the actual colour of

any Port cannot be necessarily taken as an indication either of age or quality. In order to meet the demand for a cheaper-quality Tawny wine the shipper has to blend the somewhat younger red Ports with a certain amount of white Port.

Now that I have said something about Tawny Ports and Ruby Ports let me say a word about White Ports. Their mere existence has often prompted the inquiry: "What colouring matter is used in Port?" This arises out of the belief that all Ports are white when made and are then coloured up to reach the desired standard. The truth of the matter is that there is no difference in the making of white Ports and red Ports except that white Port is made from white grapes and red Port from red grapes.

As for Vintage Port, I revere it as the greatest of all wines. It is made from a limited quantity of *the finest wine of an exceptionally fine year.* Having got that fine year, the shipper picks out the very finest of these fine wines, blends them and christens the lot "So-and-so's Vintage so-and-so year." Thus Vintage Port rightly earns the reputation of being the *crème de la crème* of Port Wine.

About a year and a half after blending the lot is shipped from Oporto to be bottled by wine merchants, as it is the function of Vintage Port to live its life and mature in bottle *in the climate in which it is to be consumed,* instead of maturing in casks in the lodges at Oporto as do the Ruby and Tawny wines, which are bottled for immediate consumption.

Vintage Port is really a very great test for a shipper, for, when deciding whether or not to ship a particular year as a Vintage, he has to stake his whole reputation on the wine and has to foretell not whether the wine is attractive when it is being made, but what it is going to turn out after, say, ten years or more in bottle.

There are some who favour the fining of Vintage Port by white of egg or some other agent before bottling. Personally I prefer to leave it unfined on the scantling to fall bright by itself, and then to bottle on a nice clear autumn day when the barometer is high and when one feels especially well oneself. The one golden rule after Vintage Port has been bottled is to allow it to remain undisturbed in its original bin until such time as the crust has formed and the wine is ready to drink.

Crust does not form in one fell swoop, but rather in a series of precipitations throughout the years; so that, if you shake up a recent precipitation before it has properly formed into a hard, clinging crust, you will throw back the particles into the wine and get a "muddy" result, with the chance that the "mud" will not always settle down again into a good firm crust. During the period when Vintage Ports are maturing in bottle they may seem very unattractive at times. But once the wine has stopped throwing its crust, and is reaching its proper maturity, it quite gets over this slight sickness.

If you feel that you cannot afford Vintage Port it is always as well to know where the next best thing can be found, and I draw your attention to Crusted Ports. These are young wines, probably a blend of several years, which have been shipped in wood and allowed to mature in bottle in the same way as Vintage Port. They are probably not up to the high degree of quality one finds in a Vintage Port, nor do they probably show the "lusciousness" and "breed" which are among the added charms of Vintage Port, but they do show the bottle flavour and are a refreshing change from the normal daily wood wines.

Vintage and Crusted Ports are, of course, dessert wines, good for drinking at the end of a meal and after it. Tawny Port is the wine one can drink at almost any time of the day: being lighter in body, it is an excellent pick-me-up with a biscuit in mid-morning.

Consider the variety of Port. In a Ruby wine one will not expect to find the particular qualities of bouquet and flavour that one would look for in a Crusted Port—and expect in greater measure still in a Vintage wine. Ruby Port has the freshness and grape-like sweetness of youth, and its bouquet has something of the natural aroma of the grape still lingering in it. In a Tawny Port you will look for more delicacy and less body, and a good deal less of the natural grape in the bouquet. A really good Tawny Port will have a matured balance and a touch of elegance. A good Crusted Port will have more depth, greater fullness and "bottle flavour."

Still greater are the delights of a Vintage Port of a really great year: in the bouquet are what might be called overtones and undertones—a roundness and depth—and the wine on the palate forms a splendid harmony, with a finesse and a wonderfully balanced sweetness that do not cloy. Those who have given Port little thought might imagine the only gradations in wine are those of quality, from poor to excellent. There is in fact an immense variety in Port, and the more one studies it with affectionate care the more delicate the nuances one will find in the different types and vintages—and in the search for them there is great interest and delight.

To show you that Port Wine is a living thing, may I mention one of the curious features of the working of nature. It is a fact that, whenever the sap rises or falls in the vine, which occurs twice a year during the equinoctial periods at the end of September and the end of March, Port Wines are sometimes known to go out of condition for a short time. One would think that, being in bottle in a cellar of even temperature, they would be immune from this reaction, but they are not, and the lesson we learn from this is that we should be specially careful of all Port Wines about these two periods.

Beware of Imitations! It is sometimes claimed that the public believe that Port is the name of any fortified wine that is red and sweet, and, although much confusion arises in the mind of the public from such expressions as "Port type" or "Port style," may I remind you once again that Port cannot be made anywhere outside the Douro district of Portugal and must be shipped, with the necessary Certificate of Origin issued by the Portuguese authorities, over the bar of the River Douro to the various world-markets: so be on your guard against wines offered as Port which are, in fact, not Port.

To one without some experience, choosing Port Wine in a restaurant is not so easy, but don't let anyone be put off by a wine waiter who, with all the wiles at his disposal, is trying to push a certain line on his list. To all younger people I would say: Read a little about wine so that at any rate you have a basic knowledge; have a regular wine merchant with whom you can talk wine, and you can enter a restaurant feeling that you are in a position to choose the wine that suits both your palate and your pocket.

May I add a few words about decanting Port in one's home. So many have asked how long should a wine be decanted before use. No hard-and-fast rules can be laid down, except that a very old Vintage Port requires less time to breathe after being decanted than a younger wine. Generally speaking, I have found it best to stand up the bottle of Vintage Port on the morning of the day one intends to drink it, and on one's return home in the evening it can safely be decanted. The finest of Vintage Ports will begin to deteriorate twenty-four hours after decanting, but Ruby and Tawny Port will stand up much longer to contact with the air—perhaps a week.

If one has a very old bottle of Vintage Port, and one is not quite certain of the cork, a good way is to knock the head off the bottle. This is quite easily done and obviates the necessity for heating tongs. Simply place the corkscrew through the cork, after having removed all traces of wax or capsule, then stand the bottle upright and grip it by the base. Take a good strong carving knife, and holding the carving knife *lightly* swing it up sharply along the side of the neck where the top of the bottle has a slight flange. After two or three pendulum strokes it will be found that the top of the neck will be cleanly cut, and the cork can easily be removed by drawing the corkscrew. It is remarkable how easily this small operation can be completed, but remember to hold the carving knife lightly: if held firmly, one is inclined to break the bottle at the base of the neck.

Talking of decanting, I am reminded of an amusing little

episode which occurred some twenty-five years ago when I was dining with my late cousin, Ernest Cockburn, in a Midland town. My cousin was a great connoisseur of Port Wine and in addition he was a man of commanding presence. I remember we had a delicious dinner with some delightful wines, and to end up with my cousin had ordered a bottle of Vintage Port. This was brought to the table in a basket-cradle by a boy of very small stature with a very large apron tied around his waist. My cousin glared at him and asked:

"Have you shaken the bottle, my boy?"

"No, sir," replied the youth, "but I will." And he did!

I shall never forget the look of consternation on my cousin's face; but, being a man with a very great sense of humour and ready wit, he immediately saw the funny side and we both collapsed with laughter. The pink-faced youth was given a short talk on how to decant Port Wine and then departed with some silver coins in his hand and a contented look on his face. I don't suppose he ever committed that heinous crime again!

As to glasses, there is a useful little adage which goes as follows: the bigger the cask the better the wine, the bigger the bottle the better the drinking—and this also applies in a modified degree to glasses. I hate drinking Port Wine out of a thimble glass, and if you ask the wine waiter to bring you a Port glass and then double it, you will be getting somewhere nearer the right measure.

Recent Vintages. Very often one is asked which is the best year among recent Vintages. Excluding the 1908s and 1912s, both of which were exceptionally fine, I would say without any hesitation that the wine of this century so far is 1927. This Vintage has just about reached the peak of its perfection. It was followed by the 1934s and 1935s, both of which were very good indeed. The 1947 and 1948 vintages were also shown by some of the shippers: and the vintage of 1950 was "declared" (i.e., announced as a vintage year) by some, but it will be a number of years yet before any of them will be ready for drinking. For those, however, who have a little spare money left after the tax-collector has taken his fill, I would strongly recommend that a good investment for a wine-lover would be any recent vintages of well-known shippers.

PORT SHIPPERS

About eighty firms ship Port to Britain, and the following are among the best known. Editor.

Barros Almeida
Butler and Nephew
Calem
Campbell and Menzies
Cockburn Smithes
Croft
Da Silva
Delaforce
Dow (Silva and Cozens)
Ferreira
Fuerheerd
Fonseca
Gonzalez, Byass
Gould, Campbell

Graham
Hunt Roope
Kopke
Martinez Gassiot
Morgan
Offley
Ramos Pinto
Robertson Bros.
Sandeman
Smith Woodhouse
Taylor
Tuke Holdsworth
Van Zellers
Warre

SOME PORT VINTAGES SINCE 1896

1896 Excellent	1924 Good	1954 Some good
1897 Very good	1927 Excellent	wines
1900 Light but	1934 Very good	1955 Very good
excellent	1935 Very good·	1958 Good; light
1904 Good	1945 Excellent	1960 Very good
1908 Very fine	1947 Very good	1963 Very good
1912 Excellent	1948 Very good	1966 Excellent
1917 Good	1950 Light; of high	1967 Very good
1920 Good	quality	1970 Excellent
1922 Good		

XI · MADEIRA

BY A. J. B. RUTHERFORD

MADEIRA has fallen out of fashion and by many people is completely unknown; which is a pity, because good Madeira, old Madeira, is one of the most remarkable wines in the world and has its place in the scheme of wine-drinking and appreciation.

Madeira is made in the island of that name from white grapes pressed in the traditional manner and fermented in casks like most other wines.

What gives Madeira its characteristic flavour and its property of extreme longevity is the fact that the grapes are grown on volcanic soil enriched by the ashes of forests destroyed by fire centuries ago, and the fermented grape-juice is heated at a moderate temperature for several months in what is known as an *estufa*.

This process takes away the original acidity from the wine and imparts to it a burnt, bitter sweetness difficult to describe but unmistakable.

Another result of this process is that Madeira, unlike most

other wines, rarely throws much sediment in bottle, and therefore does not suffer the usual decay. In fact, the most noticeable result of keeping Madeira many years in bottle is that instead of deteriorating it gets more and more concentrated, with a heavy, pronounced "bottle flavour" which is very attractive.

Also following from this we find that Madeira is not so susceptible to heat and cold as many other wines. Madeira is improved by heat and is not affected by cold, which accounts for the fact that the chief markets for it are India and Scandinavia, and, in the old days, Russia.

In Britain, Madeira has to compete with the two other strong wines, Sherry and Port, and comes off a poor third. One of the reasons is undoubtedly the fact that the present-day consumer does not know when to drink it or what sort to choose. The fact of the matter is that it can be used as a change for either.

There are four main types of Madeira, called after the species of grape from which they are made: Bual, Malmsey, Sercial, Verdelho.

Bual and Verdelho are the two most popular types in Britain because they are not too expensive and are the dessert wines. Being a white wine, Madeira can be drunk with much pleasure after Champagne when many people prefer not to drink Port.

Sercial is a dry wine and it is never cheap because only a small quantity is made: it makes a very pleasant pre-prandial drink, particularly in cold weather.

Malmsey is a very sweet wine of superb quality which is much in favour in Scandinavian countries. It is mostly too sweet to be popular in Britain, but when Malmsey is really very old it is perhaps the finest wine in the world and probably the longest lived.

The best Malmsey is grown on vines quite close to the seashore, while most of the others grow on little terraces built up the sides of extremely steep hills.

There is now no "Vintage Madeira." It is made on the *solera* system as is Sherry. This means that the casks are stored in rows according to their age, and the style and type are kept constant by replacing each year what has been withdrawn by wines of the same type. When a Madeira bottle label bears a year it indicates the date when the *solera* was begun, and while there may be a small proportion of wine of that age in the blend it has come to mean little more than a brand.

The island of Madeira is extremely small, approximately thirty-six miles long by seventeen miles wide, with a range of mountains along the centre up to 6,000 ft. high. Actually the chief products are not wine but sugar and bananas, and the space left for growing wine is quite small. The vines are grown on pergolas, and the grapes are picked from underneath. Owing to the really mountainous country the juice, when pressed in the local press-house, is carried down to the wine lodges in goatskins, where it is emptied into casks for fermenting and maturing.

Because of the difficulty of production and the small quantity produced, Madeira can never become a popular wine for the general public; it has a much more specialist role.

The island, one of the most beautiful places in the world, with a mean average temperature of 70 deg. F. all the year round, produces one of the loveliest of all wines—but it has to be selected carefully. One must not buy the cheapest wine that happens to be labelled Madeira and expect to enjoy it. Deal with someone you can trust: which is good advice in buying any wine, but is supremely important with Madeira. Do not choose too heavy or too sweet a wine. Choose a medium light Bual or a golden Verdelho. Make sure the wine has been at least two years in bottle before you draw the cork, and you will find it is the wine you have been looking for. Shooting, fishing, hunting, walking, motoring, in hot weather, in cold weather, with a biscuit in the middle of the morning, at the end of lunch or dinner, its brilliant dark-golden colour and pungent luscious bouquet cannot fail to give you pleasure.

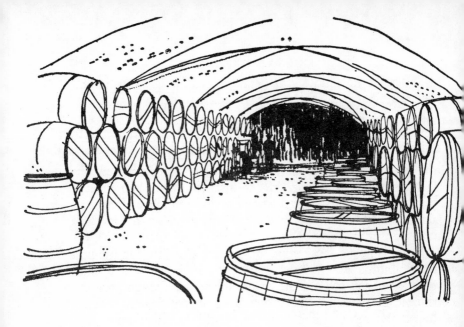

XII · COGNAC BRANDY

BY FREDERICK HENNESSY

WHEREVER in the world grapes will grow with sufficient ease and abundance to justify the making of wine it is equally possible to distil these wines into Brandy. Why then has the word COGNAC become synonymous with the finest of all Brandies?

For the answer it is necessary first to look back over four hundred years to a time when the farmers of the Charente—a county of France lying east of the Bay of Biscay—were finding difficulty in storing their over-abundant and unsold wines.

A Dutch apothecary who happened to be travelling to the near-by port of La Rochelle grew interested in their plight. He taught them the simple fact that alcohol will boil and pass off into vapour at a lower temperature than water, and that by boiling alcohol and condensing this vapour they would retain the very heart of their wine and, at the same time, reduce its volume to approximately one-tenth of the original —thus bringing about a great saving in casks, storage and

126

shipping space. For want of a better name he called this product Burnt Wine—Brandjwyn in Dutch—and this word has gradually developed into Brandy.

In the centre of the vineyards where these farmers make their wine lies the historic old town of Cognac, and from it the district has derived its name. The apothecary left the farmers of the Cognac district to discover during the ensuing years that, by the strange coincidence of a number of circumstances, they had fallen upon a liquid so precious that its fame was soon to spread to the four corners of the earth.

What is it that these *vignerons* have learned during the past four hundred years? First, perhaps, that because of a combination of soil and climate their wine, which though pleasant, showed no particular merit, has been proved beyond a doubt to be the most suitable in the world for distillation into Brandy.

Then they have learned that the somewhat antiquated pot still, which the apothecary originally taught them to use, has never been improved upon for sheer quality. Though modern apparatus will show more economical results, it is only the old-time pot still which will retain in distillation those characteristics of the wine that eventually develop into the delicious bouquet for which fine Cognac is so famous.

They have learned that certain vineyards within their district (now bearing legally defined boundaries) produce more suitable wine than others. The most famous of these vineyards lie on the chalky soil known as La Grande Champagne. Hence the expression "Fine Champagne" Cognac.

In the Cognac district the soil is not rich and the climate can be treacherous; half the growth of a vineyard is often carried away by frost and mildew before the grapes can be harvested. But just as man thrives on adversity, so it seems does wine. And when wines are put to trial by fire in the form of distillation, only those of true character emerge with honour.

But now this fiery young spirit must be mellowed and tamed by long and patient years in cask. Only by allowing Brandy to breathe in a cask of oak can the by-products of the wine develop and the liquid take on its rich golden colour. Once bottled this process will cease and the Brandy will acquire no further "age."

And so, in the Cognac district, it is still the farmer who, with the experience of many generations behind him, distils the wine into Brandy. There are over four thousand of these small distillers, but very few have either the space or the capital to keep their Brandy for maturation. The majority, therefore, sell their newly distilled Brandies to one or other of the great shipping houses, most of whom own distilleries and possess not only the accommodation but also the world-wide organization necessary for distribution.

Some of the large shipping houses will offer Vintage Brandy to the export markets for maturing privately, but the majority prefer to build up a large and varied stock, which they will mature themselves. This is necessary for the continuity of their usual blends which they offer to the world under the label of a THREE STAR, a V.S.O.P., etc.

It is well to remember, however, that these symbols, such as THREE STAR, set no common standard. Their significance depends on the quality, the age and the size of the stocks of each individual shipper. And it is to the name of the shipper that the seeker of good Brandy should look for his guarantee.

As in all things, your choice of Cognac must be guided first and foremost by your own palate. But the palate itself sometimes welcomes guidance. At an early age, my own was fortunate enough to receive such guidance from a venerable and eloquent old gentleman with a great knowledge and love of human nature. He described a fine Cognac as he would a beautiful and intelligent woman, whose charm is tender without being insipid, bringing with it a feeling of stimulation and leaving behind a sense of sweet satisfaction. With the intolerance of youth I may have considered this description somewhat flowery, but thinking of it now I can find no truer or more subtle comparison.

SOME TYPICAL BOTTLES AND GLASSES

While there is no hard-and-fast rule nowadays about the shape of wine glasses, those shown above are all in general use. An untinted glass of medium size with the lip narrowing a little may be used for any wine. For red wines and Brandy the glass should be so thin that the wine or spirit can, if necessary, be gently warmed by the hand.

HCW—E

Beware, therefore, of insipid sweetness in a Brandy, for there will be no genuine or mature character in such softness. In the same way the aftertaste may bring with it regrets.

Beware of the dust and cobwebs surrounding the bottle "discovered" in a long-forgotten cellar, for they may disguise a Brandy which ceased to live and breathe in cask at all-too-early a stage in its career.

Do not conclude that because a Brandy is dark brown in colour that it must be old; the tint may come from the addition of caramel.

Look through the label to the liquid behind, and trust the good name of the shipper.

Do not think it sacrilege to add water, or soda if you will, to a young and vigorous Cognac Brandy, for the strength of its character will refresh your body and soul.

Do not seek among the goldfish bowls for a suitable glass. Certainly an inverted shape will tend to retain the bouquet, but let it be of a size which you can warm in the palm of the hand, and so help to release that natural and delicious fragrance which is the very heart of wine.

a *a* *a*

A NOTE ON ARMAGNAC

BY H. WARNER-ALLEN

ARMAGNAC BRANDY, grown and distilled in that region of Gascony which lies inland between Bordeaux and the Pyrenees, is a fine spirit which has every right to be judged by its own standards.

Armagnac and Cognac have one thing in common, they are both distilled from wine. That wine used to be grown from the same vine, but even in this respect they are drifting apart. Armagnac on the whole remains true to the traditional grape, the Folle Blanche or Picpoul, but Cognac depends more and

more on the Saint-Émilion grape. Their methods of distillation
are poles apart. Armagnac is distilled only once, in a continuous flow, and at a much lower alcoholic degree than Cognac.
There is a far wider margin for local distinctions arising from
the peculiarities of the wines employed, and the lower strength
of Armagnac leaves room for a great variety in taste and smell.

It is a commonplace in Cognac that Brandy owes half its
taste and should owe all its colour to the wood in which it is
matured. Armagnac is no less dependent on the wood for its
qualities, and it is peculiarly fortunate in the local variety of
black oak which might have been expressly created for the
storage of its *eaux-de-vie*. Armagnac casks are hewn, for the
saw would release an excess of juices from the heart of
the trunk.

Under its influence—the timber is lined with black
veins and studded with black knots—Armagnac matures and
colours with such speed that the Brandies exported from
Cognac to Scandinavia are aged by the addition of young
Armagnacs. The district known as Bas-Armagnac produces by
far the finest Brandies, and their variety is remarkable. The
Marquis de Montesquiou, a descendant of d'Artagnan, has
blended some of the lighter spirits for use in a long drink,
and their freedom from sugar gives them a stimulating freshness and makes them mix excellently with water or soda.
Then there is a scale of fine Armagnacs of notable age with
exceedingly rich and complex bouquet and taste, rustic and
rollicking as compared with the ethereal refinement of great
Cognac, yet delightful and clinging to the glass as no other
perfume does.

In the United Kingdom more than two dozen agents deal
in Armagnac, and a wine merchant will readily be able to
obtain a few bottles for you at a reasonable price. Vintage years
count little, as good *eau-de-vie* is made in nearly every vintage.

SOME COGNAC SHIPPERS

Of more than one hundred and fifty shippers of Cognac the following are among the best known in Great Britain. Editor.

Barnett and Elichagaray	Hennessy
Bisquit Dubouché	Hine
Camus	Martell
Castillon	Monnet
Courvoisier	Normandin
Cusenier	Otard
Delamain	Pellisson
Denis Mounie	Prunier
Exshaw	Remy Martin
Frapin	Robin, Jules
Gautier	Rouyer, Guillet & Co.
Godet	Salignac

COGNAC VINTAGES

The dates of the great Cognac vintages are of little more than academic interest to most people, but one will occasionally find an old brandy bottled with a vintage date, such as 1906. The very old brandies are usually refreshed from time to time by the addition of brandy of similar quality, but from the time the brandy is bottled no improvement takes place. The letters V.S.O.P. mean Very Special Old Pale, but brandy shippers have often symbols of their own to indicate that the brandy is of special quality, and it will almost always be a blend of different vintage years.

BUYING AND STORING WINE

BY AUGUSTUS MUIR

1. Treat Wine With Care

THE storing of wine is a hard problem for many people. Not every house has a cellar, and not every cellar is suitable for wine.

The place where wine is kept should have a temperature that does not stray, in winter or summer, below 50 deg. Fahrenheit or above 60 deg. The ideal is a steady 55 deg. If you store a fine wine in too cold or too hot an atmosphere it will suffer. It will suffer even more if it is subject to alternate chilling and heating. The temperature of a cellar or a wine-cupboard is a vital matter.

Wine must be stored in the dark, and it must be safe against vibration.

Wine-racks for storage can be bought; they can also be made.

Wine that cannot be accommodated at home will usually be stored by the wine merchant without cost. But be sure to

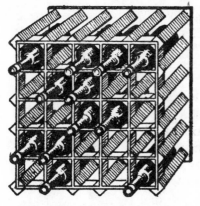

*Wine-rack for storing bottles
on their sides*

have your older wine delivered at home some time before you propose to open it; a wine that has thrown a deposit may take weeks to settle down, and Port with crust may need six months.

It goes without saying that wine should always be stored horizontally; if it rests upright so that the bubble of air is at the cork, the cork may dry out and shrink—and the wine may deteriorate.

Spirit bottles, on the other hand, should be left standing upright lest the cork should suffer from contact with alcohol of twice the strength contained in Port or Sherry.

2. Notes on Equipment

Cradle. Wine poured from a bottle that lies in a wine-basket keeps flowing back and stirring up the deposit. Never use a basket for serving wine, but it can be very useful in decanting, whether it be of the Claret or Burgundy pattern.

Corkscrew. Make sure you have a corkscrew with wide spirals; the narrow gimlet type will fail to grip a stubborn cork—and some corks can be very stubborn. If you have no leather hand-guard (not many people have, nowadays), a thick towel may save you from a cut hand in the rather unlikely event of a bottle being defective and breaking while you draw a reluctant cork.

Wine-basket or cradle

You will be well equipped if you have one of the lever-type corkscrews which call for little effort, and the double-screw type makes drawing a simple matter—provided you have put the screw straight down to the end of the cork.

If a cork has been a long time in the bottle it *may* give trouble. It may simply refuse to be drawn: or it may threaten to disintegrate. There are two ways of meeting this problem.

If you possess a pair of tongs, of which the pincers fit exactly round the neck of a wine bottle, heat them until they are just short of being red-hot. The best way is to make them cherry-red, then wait about a minute, and place them gently round the neck of the bottle at the foot of the cork; leave them for a few moments, then remove them. At once draw round the neck a feather or a

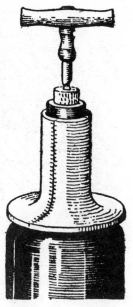

Old-fashioned hand-guard in position. A folded towel may be used instead

piece of rag dipped in cold water, and the neck will come neatly away with the wretched cork enclosed.

Mr. Frederick Cockburn, in his chapter on Port, describes another way which needs skill and confidence — that of knocking the head off the bottle with a carving knife.

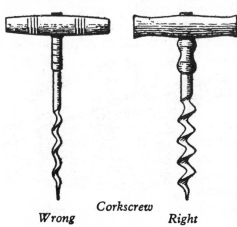

Wrong   **Corkscrew**   *Right*

Wine Funnel. For use in decanting, the funnel should not be of metal. A convenient plastic one can be readily procured. Some people always strain the wine in decanting; and as a filter in the funnel a piece of fine muslin cannot be bettered, but it is well to wring it out several times in warm water to make sure it has not the faintest odour or taint, even of the soap in which it was last washed.

Heating tongs for cutting neck cleanly when a cork is old and obstinate, or likely to disintegrate

3. Glasses and Decanters

A wineglass has several functions. To display the colour of the wine so that it is a pleasure to the eye. To permit you to enjoy the bouquet. To be a comely thing in itself, worthy of holding wine and easy to drink from.

To display the colour the glass must be clear. Coloured glass was popular in the days when many white wines were apt to be cloudy, and a tinted wineglass was a convenient camouflage.

To contain and thus accentuate the bouquet of the wine the best type of glass narrows slightly at the rim. Moreover, the glass itself must be thin, so that the warmth of the hand can be imparted to a red wine. In his chapter on Cognac Mr. Frederick Hennessy has exploded the idea that only a vast balloon glass is appropriate to a fine Brandy.

The decanter ought to be of clear glass; a well-shaped decanter with wine in it is one of the most simply beautiful things the eye of a wine-lover can rest upon.

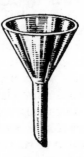

Decanting funnel

May I suggest that you acquire, when the opportunity arises, a small decanter which will hold exactly half a bottle of wine. It may be that you wish to drink only half a bottle of *ordinaire* one evening, and it is not always possible to buy the wine you require in half-bottles. A young and vigorous wine will keep for several days, particularly if you pour what is left of the bottle into a small decanter, without leaving air to cause oxydisation, and stopper it.

4. Hints on Buying Wine

"Trust your wine merchant." You will have read this advice several times in these pages. Of course, the writers assume that you have found a *good* wine merchant. There are good ones and not so good, and fortunately this is a matter in which the truth very soon comes out. (A type of wine merchant to distrust is one who is continually dealing in "bargains.") The business of many a good old-fashioned wine merchant has been bought on his death by a big firm, and sometimes a manager has been installed whose knowledge of wine is considerably less than his knowledge of business methods. He can be of little help to a beginner. You must cast about you until you find a wine merchant with knowledge, patience and sympathy—and they certainly are to be found. You might do well to have more than one wine merchant, for some specialize in one wine and some in another.

A wine merchant should know those good vintage years when wines with famous names happen to have been failures—and he should pass on to you the information. Even among the great First Growths of Claret, for example, there have been years when one or other of these four vineyards has not produced a first-class wine.

In buying wine, remember that if you make your order up to a dozen bottles the wine will usually be packed and transported to your door, free of charge. Many wine merchants will perform a similar service with a package containing a minimum of three bottles of spirits.

Just as much care is needed in the choice of a wine for everyday use as of a fine wine for some special occasion. Among lower-priced wines it would be foolish to ignore the wines of South Africa and Australia. Two-thirds of the wine drunk in Britain today has been made in local factories from imported grape-must, etc., and I would be the last person to say that "British wines" are unwholesome; they have their place and supply a need, but you cannot expect them to have the qualities of wine from the European vineyards. What we are apt to forget is that the cheaper the wine the greater the percentage of overheads. When you pay £1.50 for a bottle of wine you are getting much better value per penny than when you pay 50p. Customs duty is the same; so are bottling, transport, wages and all the other items that must be added to the basic cost of the wine. A better cork may be used for the better wine, but not a better bottle, nor a better lorry chosen for its transport. This aspect of value-for-money in wine-buying is worth considering.

Whatever wine you may specialize in, I would urge you to widen your experience as much as possible. Not many men have drunk a greater variety of wine than Professor Saintsbury, and in his *Notes on a Cellar Book* he made it plain that, of many of the wines on which he comments, he had bought only one or two bottles. Part of the varied enjoyment of wine-drinking lies in the widening of one's knowledge in a happy mood of adventure.

On page 141 I have suggested a fairly wide selection of wines for the cellar of a beginner, and it can be added to or subtracted from according to one's personal whims. As to the size of bottles, generally speaking the larger the bottle the more slowly the wine will mature and the better a good wine will become. A magnum of Claret, bottled at the same time as a half-bottle of the same wine, will almost certainly turn out in due course the finer. The opposite can be said of Brandy. The magnum of Brandy which a wine waiter may produce with a flourish is no better for having been thus bottled.

In buying still wines of fine quality it is often a problem whether one should choose wines bottled in Britain or pay the higher price demanded for those bottled at the vineyards. There are British merchants who maintain that they bottle wines with as great care and skill as will be found in any other country; but some express doubts about this.

To buy Claret with the famous legend *Mis en bouteillie au château* on its label was once a much more substantial guarantee of quality than it is now, because at some vineyards the wines are "château bottled" even in years when the wine is so poor it ought to be sold in bulk as non-vintage wine without a château name. The older vintages of château-bottled Clarets, if they can be obtained at all, are costly; the beginner might do well to concentrate on more recent vintages and wait for them to mature. As a general rule he will find that wines bottled in Britain, if supplied by a good wine merchant, can be bought with confidence.

5. Wine Shippers

The functions of a shipper include a good deal more than the mere dispatching of his wares from the port of shipment to British bonded warehouses to await clearance. The quality of the wine will in most cases depend upon the integrity of the shipper. Shippers have their traditions and their special goods and marks, and the wines sold under their names generally maintain a standard of good quality and value.

With the great wines of Bordeaux we depend upon the shipper's honesty to give us the wines which are described as Château This or That. With the more ordinary Bordeaux wines the district wines sold under names such as Médoc or St. Émilion, as well as those of parishes like Margaux or St. Julien, we must rely on the shipper giving us a good blend. But even the very great wines of Burgundy may be blended. With the majority of German wines, too, we are in the shipper's hands. And as for Port and Sherry, the name of the shipper is the first thing to look for.

I should be failing in my duty to the reader if I did not add with emphasis that there *are* good shippers whose names you will not see displayed in the advertisement columns of the daily papers. I intend no slight on those shippers who advertise widely: the very fact that they do so is a challenge to themselves to maintain the standard of their wines.

🐦 🐦 🐦

A NOTE ON ALCOHOL

NATURE has decreed that about 15 per cent of alcohol is the maximum amount which the fermentation of the grape can produce, although it is claimed that in some wine-growing regions abnormal percentages have been recorded.

It is easy to be misled about the alcoholic content of a wine. Taste is little criterion, for a thin, sharp wine may have a good deal more alcohol than one that tastes rich and sweet. Sometimes a Burgundy has over 13 per cent of alcohol, and a Rhône wine over 14 per cent, as against 9 per cent or less for many an *ordinaire*. The use of the name "Bordeaux" on a wine label is now controlled by French law; and, apart from other qualifications, a red wine thus labelled must contain 9·75 per cent of alcohol. The greater Sauternes often have over 14 per cent, and to qualify for the name "Sauternes" they must have at least 12·5 per cent. A "Médoc" and a "Graves" need only have 10 per cent, but to qualify for the name "Graves Supérieures" wines must have a minimum of 12 per cent.

Some of the greater Hocks imported into Britain have as much as 13 per cent, but Moselle has seldom more than 11 per cent. Champagne generally has from 11 per cent to 14 per cent, and many Italian wines have 14 per cent of alcohol.

On the label of an ordinary bottle of spirits you may read that the alcoholic content is "70° Proof" —or "30° Under Proof," which is the same thing. Since Proof Spirit contains about 57·1 per cent of alcohol by volume it follows that full Proof Spirit is about four-sevenths alcohol and three-sevenths water. A simple calculation will show that an ordinary bottle of Whisky, Brandy or Gin contains 40 per cent of alcohol—which is almost exactly twice the amount in Port and Sherry.

A BEGINNER'S CELLAR

The following is a specimen cellar, distributed among a good variety of wines. The choice of *ordinaires* is left to the individual taste. *Editor.*

APÉRITIFS

VERMOUTH	1	bottle Italian (sweet)
	1	bottle French (dry)
SHERRY	1	bottle dry Sherry
	1	bottle dry South African
	1	bottle dry Australian
MADEIRA	1	bottle (dry)

TABLE WINES

CLARET	9	bottles of Classified and good *Bourgeois* Growths
BURGUNDY	6	bottles: Mâcon, Beaune, Pommard, Beaujolais, Corton, etc.
	3	bottles distributed between Nuits-St.-George, Chambolle-Musigny, Clos de Vougeot, or other wines of distinction
RHÔNE	2	bottles Châteauneuf-du-Pape (a heavy wine for a cold winter evening)
ITALIAN	2	flasks red Chianti
	2	bottles Barolo (full, heavy red wine)
CHAMPAGNE	2	bottles
WHITE BORDEAUX	2	bottles medium sweet—Graves or other district
	2	bottles sweet—1 Sauternes, 1 Barsac
WHITE BURGUNDY	3	bottles, one being of finer quality
GERMAN	6	bottles, two being of finer quality
ALSATIAN	2	bottles

DESSERT WINES

PORT	3	bottles—Ruby, Tawny, Crusted
SHERRY	1	bottle Oloroso or Old Brown
MADEIRA	2	bottles: one Bual, one Verdelho

BRANDY

COGNAC	1	bottle
ARMAGNAC	1	bottle

A DICTIONARY OF WINE

AND OF OTHER ALCOHOLIC LIQUORS

COMPILED BY AUGUSTUS MUIR

The names of many of the vineyards in the main wine districts of Bordeaux, Burgundy and the Rhine and Moselle will be found in the respective chapters. Editor.

ABSINTHE. A powerful spirit of which wormwood and other aromatic plants are the ingredients. It is drunk diluted with water. Prohibited in France and U.S.A.

ADVOCAAT. A Dutch liqueur made of Brandy, yolk of egg, etc.

ALCOHOL. The ethyl alcohol in wine has no colour and little smell. About 15% of alcohol is the maximum created in the fermentation of grape-juice. In natural wines the amount of alcohol generally ranges from about 8% to over 14%. Sherry and other fortified wines have about 20%. Proprietary brands of spirits have about 40%. Proof Spirit contains about 57·1% alcohol—i.e., a proportion of about four-sevenths. "30° Under Proof" means 70% Proof Spirits — i.e., 40% alcohol.

ALE. Fermented "wort" derived from processed barley and hops, and after fermentation each brewer has his own method of treating the liquor. Ale and beer are terms now practically synonymous.

ALGERIA. While most Algerian wines, red and white, lack distinction, some are pleasant beverage wines, of fairly high alcoholic strength.

ALICANTE. A red, sweet, Spanish wine once popular in the U.K.

ALSACE. Alsatian vineyards, on the lower slopes of the Vosges foothills, produce white wines, some full-bodied with aromatic bouquet. (*For varieties see page 78.*)

AMONTILLADO. A medium dry type of Sherry.

AMOROSO. A name used (but *not* in Spain) to denote a sweet Oloroso Sherry.

ANGOSTURA. A brand of "bitters" used for flavouring some drinks.

ANJOU. An area of the Maine-et-Loire *département* of France producing white wine, both sweet and dry.

AQUAVIT. A Scandinavian spirit distilled from grain or potatoes and flavoured with caraway.

ARGENTINE. Large output of wines, mostly red, not many of high quality; also some sweet dessert wines, Brandies and Vermouths.

ARMAGNAC. Brandy made in the Gers *département* in S.W. France; at its best very good, but does not rival the finest Cognac.

ARRACK. A spirit generally made from rice, palm-juice, molasses, etc., according to the country. Usually drunk by natives.

ASTI SPUMANTE. A sweet, white, sparkling wine of Italy.

AUSLESE. Applied to Hocks and Moselles, the term indicates that bunches of grapes have been specially selected for the making of the wine.

AUSTRALIA. Output includes a considerable quantity of good beverage and fortified wines.

BACARDI. A well-known brand of rum.

BARBERA. A rather heavy red Italian beverage wine.

BAROLO. One of the best of all red Italian beverage wines.

BARRIQUE. A French hogshead of from 45 to 56 gal., according to the district.

BARSAC. A *commune* south of Bordeaux producing fine white wine, generally sweet, resembling the wines of Sauternes, but with a drier finish. (*See page 46.*)

BEAUJOLAIS. A large area on the hillsides above the right bank of the Saône, producing wines rather similar to those of Mâcon but a little lighter than most Burgundies. Among the best vineyards are Juliénas, Moulin-à-Vent and Fleurie.

BEAUNE. Wines named after the old town in Burgundy, many good, some of high quality. Best known of the Côte de Beaune are Aloxe - Corton, Savigny, Pommard, Volnay, Meursault, the Montrachet wines and Santenay.

BEER. See Ale.

BEEREN-AUSLESE. A harvesting of individually selected choice grapes for making superior Hocks and Moselles.

BEESWING. A light, floating film in old bottled port which has been compared to the transparent wing of a bee. Unlike a "crust," if it passes into the decanter or glass it does not impair the wine.

BENEDICTINE. A sweet, aromatic liqueur made in Normandy since the 16th century.

BERGERAC. An area in the Dordogne east of Bordeaux producing red and white wines, the best being those of Monbazillac; the white wines are mainly sweet and full.

BEVERAGE WINES. Unfortified wines—natural wines, both red and white—suitable for drinking on ordinary occasions.

BIN. The structure or recess in a cellar in which bottles of wine are laid down and kept.

BITTERS. Sharp essences made from certain barks, etc., used to give an "edge" to a drink.

BLAYE. A canton on the right bank of the Gironde producing much red and some white wine, some of it of fair quality.

BODEGA. In Spain the name for a wine store.

BOND. Wines and spirits "in bond" are those kept by the Customs and Excise until duty has been paid; only after they are "cleared from bond" can delivery be taken.

BORDEAUX. Chief city and seaport of the *département* of the Gironde and the name that can be applied to all Gironde wines, red and white, if they reach a certain standard of excellence.

BOTTLE-SICKNESS. A malaise, mostly temporary, that may attack certain still wines after bottling.

BOTTLE-STINK. An unpleasant smell generally caused by the wine having become too old.

BOUQUET. "Perfume" is an inadequate word to describe this quality which all fine wine possesses according to its kind. The ether and essences released by the wine on contact with the air evaporate and create the bouquet.

BOURG. A seaport on the bank of the Dordogne and the name given to wines in the canton, most of which are red.

BOURGEOIS. The name applied to hundreds of good wines of the Médoc not considered fine enough to be listed among the five great growths in 1855 when the Classification was made.

BRANDY. Spirit distilled from wine. The name may be used in any country, but the name Cognac may be used only of the Brandy of the Charente, in France, and Armagnac used only of the Brandy made in the Gers *département,* under legally controlled conditions.

BREATHE. A red wine is said to "breathe" when it comes into contact with the air after the cork has been drawn.

BRISTOL MILK. The name given by some wine merchants in Bristol to a Sherry which each has blended.

BRUT. Applied to unsweetened Champagne.

BUAL. A medium-sweet dessert wine of Madeira.

BURGUNDY. Once a province of France, now the name given to the wines of Chablis, the Côte d'Or, the Côte Châlonnaise, the Côte Mâconnaise, and Beaujolais. There is less white than red wine grown, but some of it is of a high quality, with Le Montrachet leading. The characteristic Burgundy bottle has a broad base, sloping gradually up to the neck, without the shoulders characteristic of the Bordeaux bottle.

BUTT. A cask containing 108 gal.

CABERNET. A grape from which red wines are made, the best kind being the Cabernet Sauvignon.

CABINET. A name once applied to the finest Hocks and Moselles, which were supposed to be kept in a special locked cabinet in a cellar.

CACAO. *Crème de Cacao* is a sweet liqueur with a flavour of vanilla and chocolate. A district in Venezuela claims to make the finest quality.

CALIFORNIA. Large quantities of red and white wines of many types and qualities are produced.

CALVADOS. A Brandy distilled from Normandy cider.

CANARY. Red and white wines from the Canary Islands, once popular but now rarely seen in Britain.

CANTENAC. A *commune* of the

Médoc producing Claret of high quality, including Château Brane - Cantenac, a Second Growth, and seven other Classified Growths, as well as a number of good *Bourgeois* wines.

CAPRI. Gives its name to wines, mostly white, grown on Capri, Ischia and the mainland around Naples.

CASSIS. A cordial with a flavour of black-currants which can be taken neat as a liqueur, diluted as a long drink, or used for sweetening.

CÈRONS. A district on the left bank of the Garonne, specializing in white wines which are highly perfumed, full-bodied, fairly high in alcohol. Wines of the *communes* of Podensac and Illats may use the name.

CHABLIS. This French town in the *département* of Yonne gives its name to a small output of excellent white wines. The name has been used—or mis-used—for wines of a similar type but inferior to the genuine Chablis.

CHAI. A French storage place above ground for wine in cask, not to be confused with an underground cellar.

CHAMBERTIN. Red Burgundy from the Chambertin vineyards in the *commune* of Gevrey-Chambertin on the Côte de Nuits.

CHAMBOLLE-MUSIGNY. A *commune* on the Côte de Nuits that gives its name to some excellent red Burgundies, including Les Musigny.

CHAMBRER. The French word *chambre* (room) gives its name to the gentle and natural process of bringing a red wine up to a pleasant temperature by removing it from the cellar (the ideal temperature of which is 55° F.) and allowing it to stand for a suitable length of time in a warmer atmosphere.

CHAMPAGNE. The most famous sparkling wine in the world took its name from the French province where it was made. The name must not be confused with the Grande Champagne and Petite Champagne districts of the Charente where the finest Cognac is distilled.

CHAPTALISATION. The process (named after its inventor, Chaptal) by which wines which might have been inferior in stamina are helped to attain a higher alcoholic content by the addition of sugar at vintage time. Since it is forbidden by law in the Gironde, no Claret is a chaptalised wine.

CHARTREUSE. An aromatic liqueur originally made at the Carthusian monastery of the Grande Chartreuse, near Grenoble in France. The green type is higher in alcohol and less sweet than the yellow.

CHÂTEAU. As part of the name of a wine the word is found mostly in the Gironde, with *Cru de* and *Domaine de* as variants.

CHÂTEAU BOTTLED. *Mis en bou-*

teille au château or *Mis en bouteille du château* on the label of a bottle means that the wine was made from grapes grown in the named vineyard and bottled by the proprietor.

CHÂTEAUNEUF-DU-PAPE. A well-known, rather heavy table wine, mostly red, of fairly high alcoholic content, grown in the Rhône valley near Avignon.

CHERRY BRANDY. A liqueur derived from fermented cherry juice which had contained a carefully measured proportion of crushed cherry stones to give the characteristic bitter-almond flavour; nowadays it is also made synthetically.

CHIANTI. The most famous of the Italian wines, made in the province of Siena. The wine, mostly red, is bottled in an attractive straw-covered flask known as a *fiasco*.

CHILE. Next to Argentina, this republic is the largest producer of red and white wines in South America, and its wines are generally of a higher quality than those of the Argentine.

CLARET. The name given to the red wines of Bordeaux. The name is derived, it is believed, from the old word *clairet*, applied to a clear light-red Bordeaux wine. The characteristic Claret bottle has high shoulders which distinguish it from a Burgundy bottle.

COBBLERS. An American term for drinks mixed with certain proportions of wines, spirits, fruit-juices, etc.

COBLENZ. The centre of the Rhine Wine trade.

COINTREAU. A French liqueur with an orange flavour.

"CORKED!" The exclamation is usually made on those rare occasions when, on opening a bottle, it is found that the wine is tainted by degeneration of the cork.

CORSÉ. *Corsé* means that a wine is full-bodied, with good alcoholic strength and flavour.

CÔTE. As a wine term, Côte means sloping lands on which vineyards have been planted. Côte de Nuits and Côte de Beaune, where fine Burgundies are grown, together form the Côte d'Or. Côte Châlonnaise and the Côte Mâconnaise lie to the south. On the Rhône, south of Lyons, is the Côte Rôtie. In the Gironde are the Côtes de Bourg, Côtes de Blaye, etc.

CRÈME. Implying, in the names of liqueurs, a high degree of sweetness.

CRU. The French word for growth, *cru* is used of a vineyard or a group of vineyards that have some point of similarity in their wines. In the Gironde about sixty of the reputedly best wines of the Médoc were in 1855 divided into five groups, from *le premier* to *le cinquième cru*, a "Classification" still respected.

CRUST. A film-like deposit thrown by some red wines in bottle, Port in particular.

CURAÇAO. Originally a Dutch

liqueur made from Curaçao oranges and Gin or Brandy, it is now made in many countries from varying recipes.

CUVÉE. From the French *cuver*, to ferment. *Cuve* is a vat. *Cuvée* is used in various ways. *Vin de Cuvée* is from a first (and best) pressing of the grapes. A *cuvée* can mean a quantity of one particular wine in bottle.

CYPRUS. The island made wine in the days of the Roman Empire, and still produces millions of gallons, some of good but not outstanding quality, as well as Brandy.

DECANTING. The wine that has thrown a crust or deposit should be carefully decanted (through a strainer if necessary) so that the wine in the glass may be crystal clear.

DEMIJOHN. A large glass container holding several gallons of wine or spirits, usually covered with wicker to reduce the chance of breakage.

DEMI-SEC. Usually applied to Champagne; the term means half-dry, and is intended to imply that the wine is moderately sweet.

DOURO. A river which flows through Portugal and joins the Atlantic beside the town of Oporto. The finest Port is made on the hill slopes above the Upper Douro, between the Spanish frontier and Regoa.

DRY. Dry or *sec* applied to wine means the opposite of sweet. The relative significance of the word in connexion with different wines must be carefully weighed.

DUBONNET. A French *apéritif* based upon red wine with vegetable flavourings.

ENTRE-DEUX-MERS. A large area between the French rivers Garonne and Dordogne, producing a considerable quantity of white wines and some red. Only the white wines are entitled to the name of Entre-Deux-Mers.

FAREWELL. To say that a wine has a good "farewell" (or finish or after-flavour) means that its final effect on the palate is pleasant. A wine may be excellent in many respects, but without a good finish no wine can win complete approbation.

FINESSE. An elusive and charming quality of refined breeding which raises a wine above the ordinary standard of its particular type.

FINING. The process of making a wine clear in cask before bottling. The white of egg, or other substance used, forms a film that sinks to the bottom with floating particles.

FINO. A clean, dry, delicate Sherry.

FLIERS. The tiny pale particles that sometimes settle at the bottom of a bottle of white wine; they do not usually impair the taste, and often disappear after the wine has rested for a time.

FLOR. This Spanish word for "flower" indicates the yeast that grows on and covers the surface of newly fermented Sherry and enables the wine to develop some of its special characteristics.

FORTIFIED. Wines are described as "fortified" if in the process of making they have been strengthened by the addition of wine-spirits. Port, Sherry and Madeira are examples.

FRAMBOISE. An Alsatian white liqueur distilled from wild fruits of the Vosges forests.

FRAPPÉ. Iced.

FRONSAC. A small district of the Gironde, on the right bank of the Dordogne, divided into Côtes de Canon Fronsac and Côtes de Fronsac, producing full-bodied red wines of rich colour.

FRONTIGNAN. A sweet French wine, brownish in colour, from the Midi.

FRUIT. A wine has "fruit" when it has notable aroma and taste of fermented grape-sugar.

GIN. Derived from *genièvre*, the French word for juniper, the berries of which are used to flavour the spirit after it has been distilled from grain. Plymouth Gin is an unsweetened type, Old Tom Gin is sweetened, while each of the many London Gins has its own character.

GIRONDE. The French rivers Garonne and Dordogne meet below Bordeaux and become the Gironde, which flows into the Bay of Biscay. This is also the name of the *département* within whose borders nearly 50% of all the finer wines of France are grown. Its principal districts are Médoc, St. Émilion, Pomerol, Graves, Sauternes and Barsac.

GOLDWASSER. A highly alcoholic spirit, once made only at Danzig, flavoured with herbs and spices, and with tiny pieces of gold or gilt leaf which rise when the bottle is moved.

GRAVES. The large district that encloses Bordeaux and sweeps southward by the River Garonne, producing red and white wines. The red are of the finer quality, although the name *Graves* is usually applied to the white wine. Château Haut-Brion has been traditionally the greatest of all red Graves. (*See page 42.*)

GREECE. Greek wines have been made since the days of antiquity, and are still being made, including some pleasant sweet wines.

HERMITAGE. A district on the banks of the River Rhône, south of Lyons, producing some red and white table wines, very full in body and flavour and with considerable keeping qualities.

HOCK. The British name for Rhine Wine, once known as Rhenish. Hocks are bottled in tall, narrow, reddish-brown bottles. Some sparkling Hocks are made. (*See page 76.*)

HOGSHEAD. A hogshead of Claret or Burgundy contains 48 gal.; of Sherry 54; of Port 57; of Brandy 60; of Whisky 55.

HUNGARY. Of many red and

white wines made the greatest is Tokay Essence—more like a liqueur than a white wine. Among red table wines are Egri Bikaver and Egri Kadarka; among the white are Apczer, Somloi Furmint and the sweet, rich Tokay Aszu.

IMPERIALE. A French Claret bottle holding about eight and a half ordinary bottles of wine.

ITALY. After France, the largest wine-producing country in the world. See also Asti Spumante, Capri, Chianti, Marsala, Sardinia, Sicily.

JEROBOAM. A term without sound tradition. A so-called jeroboam of Champagne is a double magnum and holds four ordinary bottles. The English "jèroboam" may hold more.

KIRSCH. Kirsch or Kirschwasser is a colourless liqueur distilled from tiny black cherries in Germany and parts of Alsace and Switzerland.

KÜMMEL. A liqueur made for centuries in Holland and later in other countries, flavoured with caraway seeds and sweetened.

LAGAR. In Spain, a large trough in which grapes for making Sherry are pressed. Used also in Portugal.

LIEBFRAUMILCH. Hocks so named are of varying quality. Liebfrauenstift is now the name under which is sold the genuine wine of the Liebfrauenkirche vineyards.

LITRE. The French standard measure equal to slightly more than 1¾ British pints.

LOUPIAC. A small district on the right bank of the Garonne, opposite Barsac, producing white wines of moderate distinction, with a sweet flavour and fairly high in alcohol.

MADEIRA. The island gives its name to fortified wines of great repute. (*For varieties see page 124.*)

MADERISÉ. *Maderisé* is used of white wines that have turned deep yellow with age, the sugar being largely gone. Sometimes used to describe the objectionable smell of any wine that has been kept too long.

MAGNUM. A bottle holding two "reputed" quarts. Three magnums contain 1 gal. of wine.

MALAGA. A fortified wine made in Andalusia and shipped from the seaport of Malaga; it is very sweet, with potent bouquet and a dark-golden colour, and is more popular in France than in the U.K.

MALMSEY. A fine very sweet Madeira wine.

MANZANILLA. A very pale dry Sherry, with a characteristic and quickly recognizable flavour, which is grown in the San Lucar district.

MARASCHINO. A liqueur, once distilled only from the fermented juice of Marasca cherries grown near the seacoast of Yugoslavia; it is now made in many countries.

MARC. A rough spirit distilled either from grape husks after the making of the wine or from apple-pulp after the cider has been made.

MARGAUX. A *commune* of the Médoc which produces much good Claret and a considerable quantity that is excellent. Château Margaux itself is classified as a First Growth.

MARSALA. A fortified wine from Sicily, often drunk as an *apéritif*.

MEAD. Fermented honey that has been diluted with water. There are many recipes for making this old English beverage.

MÉDOC. The Haut-Médoc is a strip of land some thirty miles long beside the Gironde, and about six miles wide, and produces a greater quantity of superb wine than any piece of land of the same size in the world; within its *communes* are all the sixty classified growths of Claret except the Château Haut-Brion, which is in Graves. The Bas-Médoc to the north produces many good wines of *Bourgeois* quality. (*For Classified Growths see page 31.*)

MEURSAULT. White Burgundies of this district are second only to those of Montrachet.

MIDI. Red and white wines from the *départements* of Hérault, Gard and Aude, the three largest wine-producing *départements* of France, and linked together as *Vins du Midi*. They supply the national demand for *vins ordinaires*.

MONTILLA. A fine dry type of Sherry, grown in the Montilla mountains inland from Jerez. It might be called the prototype of Amontillado.

MONTRACHET. Le Montrachet is the finest of all the white Burgundies; twenty acres on the Côte d'Or contain its vineyards.

MOSELLE. Moselle (or Mosel) gives its name to the German wines grown in vineyards in the valley of that river, and of the Saar and Ruwer near their junction with it. There are good sparkling Moselles as well as still. Moselle has tall green bottles. (*See page 76.*)

MULLED WINE. Almost any full, non-vintage red wine may be used for this sovereign remedy against chill or depression. Dissolve sugar in a little water that is heating in a pan, then add wine and bring to the boil, serving with a sprinkling of grated nutmeg or other spice according to taste. Some add a beaten egg, others a dash of Brandy.

MUSCATEL. A sweet, sparkling wine.

MUST. Juice of grapes before it has fermented.

NATURE. Applied to Champagne, this word means that the wine has not been sweetened and is of the most dry type.

NEGUS. An old-fashioned drink made with Port, boiling water, sugar, lemon, grated nutmeg or other spice.

NEUCHÂTEL. A Swiss canton producing some pleasant red and white wines.

NUITS. Côte de Nuits forms the

northern portion of the Côte d'Or, where the finest Burgundies are grown. Among the Nuits wines best known in the U.K. are those of Chambertin (including Clos de Bèze); Morey (including Clos de Tart); Chambolle-Musigny (including Romanée-Conti, Richebourg and La Tâche); and Nuits-St.-Georges.

ŒIL DE PERDRIX. Meaning "the eye of a partridge," the phrase used to describe the occasional faint pink tinge of Champagne or a white Burgundy—particularly Meursault.

OIDIUM. A parasitic fungus that sometimes attacks the vine and causes great devastation.

OLOROSO. A rather full Sherry of a golden colour, the type usually met with in the U.K. being sweet.

OPORTO. The centre of the Port Wine trade on the River Douro in Portugal. The great shippers have their offices in Oporto and their lodges (wine stores) at Vila Nova de Gaia across the river.

PALATINATE. See Rheinpfalz.

PALESTINE. A wine-producing country since very ancient times; the quantity has increased and the quality improved in the last quarter of a century. The principal centre is near the seaport of Jaffa.

PALUS. The wine-growing areas alongside the Rivers Dordogne, Gironde and Garonne, with the islands in the Gironde included. The red wine grown

there is of the *ordinaire,* the *paysan* or the *artisan* type.

PASTEURIZATION. The killing of the germs or ferments in a wine by heating. Afterwards yeast is added and fermentation encouraged to start. Pasteurized wine can never attain the highest distinction.

PAUILLAC. A *commune* of the Médoc producing three of the most important wines in the world, Châteaux Lafite (now known as Lafite-Rothschild), Latour and Mouton-Rothschild, in addition to fourteen other Classified Growths and a considerable quantity of sound *Bourgeois* wine.

PEDRO JIMENEZ. A very sweet grape used for wine-making in Spain. Usually the grapes are sun-dried on straw mats before pressing, and the wine is chiefly used for sweetening good Sherries.

PERNOD. After the sale of *absinthe* was forbidden in France the firm of Pernod produced a substitute with aniseed as the foundation.

PERRY. The fermented juice of pears.

PHYLLOXERA. A plant-louse from America which attacked European vines in the latter half of the 19th century and caused great devastation, particularly in the late 'seventies and 'eighties.

PINOT. Grapes, both black and white, used in making Burgundy and Champagne.

PIQUETTE. A poor French wine made from husks of grapes

from which the juice has already been pressed. The husks are flung into a vat with water and sugar and artificially fermented with yeast.

PIPE. A Port cask of 115 gal., which should give between 56 and 57 dozen bottles.

POMEROL. A district of the Gironde adjoining St. Émilion, where the *vignerons* claim to have sacrificed quantity for quality. Of the 128 "principal growths," Château Pétrus is probably the best known. The wines are generally round and fairly full, with a pleasant, sweet, earthy hint of truffles in their bouquet. (*See page 42.*)

POMMARD. A *commune* of the Côte d'Or which produces a considerable quantity of Burgundy.

PORT. Wine grown on the hillsides of the valley of the Upper Douro, fortified with wine-spirit at vintage-time, and shipped from Oporto.

POTTLE. A wine measure that holds four Imperial pints.

POUILLY. A white Mâconnais generally known as Pouilly-Fuissé, to be distinguished from a white wine from the Loire named Pouilly-Fumé.

POURRITURE NOBLE. The "noble rottenness" of overripe sweet white grapes from which some of the finest and most luscious wines are made.

PREMIÈRES CÔTES DE BORDEAUX. A long, narrow area on the right bank of the Garonne producing some red wines of moderate quality and white wines of varying sweetness.

PROOF SPIRIT. At a temperature of 60° F., Proof Spirit contains about 57·1% of absolute alcohol by volume.

PUNCH. Old-fashioned Punch was Rum and water, with sugar and lemon, and could be taken either hot or cold. Nowadays there are many varieties.

PUNCHEON. A Brandy-cask of 120 gal., or a Rum-cask of 114 gal.

QUETSCH. An Alsatian liqueur made from the distillation of a selection of plums.

QUINTA. The Portuguese name for a vintage estate in the Douro, similar to a *château* in the Gironde.

RACKING. The process of drawing off the bright wine from one cask to another after the lees have fallen and the wine becomes clear.

REHOBOAM. A bottle so called contains eight "reputed" quarts, but the term lacks sound tradition.

REPUTED QUART. One-sixth of a gallon; thus a dozen bottles of Champagne, Burgundy or Claret contain over 2 gal. of wine. A Champagne bottle contains 80, a Burgundy 80, and a Claret 75 centilitres.

RHEINGAU. The district on the right bank of the Rhine that produces some of the finest German wines. (*See page 76.*)

RHEINPFALZ. Known as the Palatinate, this district lies a little west of the Rhine and south-west of Worms; through it runs the famous Wein Strasse some five miles in length. The Hocks of the Palatinate vary in quality from the ordinary to the magnificent. (*See page 76.*)

RHENISH HESSIA. A wine-producing district on the left bank of the Rhine. (*See page 76.*)

RHÔNE. Beside this river are many vineyards, producing wines that range from fair to good, many of them heavy and of high alcoholic content. Among the best known are Hermitage, Châteauneuf-du-Pape and Côte Rôtie.

RIESLING. Fine white grapes used for making wine in Germany, Alsace, Austria and elsewhere.

RIOJA. A region in Aragon where white and red Spanish wines are made, most of them full-bodied table wines.

ROSÉ, VIN. Pink wine which may be either still or sparkling.

RUBY PORT. A kind of Port which has not been kept long enough in cask to lose its rich ruby colour.

RUM. Spirit, of which there are three main types, distilled from molasses. Jamaican Rum is rich, Cuban is dry, and that of Trinidad and the other centres is aromatic.

SAAR. This river has many vineyards on its banks near its junction with the Mosel. Wiltingen is the greatest wine-producing *commune* in the Saar. (*See page 76.*)

STE. CROIX-DU-MONT. A commune of the Gironde *département*, on the right bank of the Garonne. It is known for its medium-sweet white wines.

ST. ÉMILION. A famous wine district in the Gironde *département*, occupying lands that look down southward upon the River Dordogne, with the city of St. Émilion in the centre. The wines have more body than the other red wines of the Gironde, with Château Cheval Blanc and Château Ausone the best among many excellent wines. (*See page 42.*)

ST. ESTÈPHE. The most northerly *commune* of the Haut Médoc where Clarets of high quality are grown. It also has a number of good *Bourgeois* wines, including Le Boscq, Phélan-Ségur, and Pomys. In the wines of St. Estèphe there is a faint and pleasant touch of astringency.

ST. JULIEN. A *commune* of the Médoc where many distinguished Clarets are produced.

SANTENAY. The most southerly *commune* of the Côte d'Or, producing some very good Burgundy and a considerable quantity that might be described as sound and pleasant.

SARDINIA. Its sweet wines include the Monica, the Nasco, the Malvasia, the Giro. Also produces a quantity of very dry table wine.

SAUMUR. The principal city in Anjou gives its name to some of the white wines of the district. Sparkling Saumur is a refreshing beverage.

SAUTERNES. On the left bank of the Garonne in the *département* of the Gironde, the district produces some of the greatest natural sweet white wines in the world, of which Château Yquem (or d'Yquem) is the most celebrated. (*See page 46.*)

SEC. This French word for dry really implies, in connexion with Champagne, that it is not so dry as the inexperienced might perhaps expect. It means sweeter than *brut* or *nature*. It is, of course, sweeter than *Extra Sec,* but not as sweet as *demi-sec.* ("*Triple-sec*" is the name of a Curaçao liqueur.)

SERCIAL. An admirable dry Madeira, made from Sercial grapes.

SÈVE. The French word for sap, when used of a wine implies that it is made from the finest of grapes and has qualities in which sweetness and vinous essences play a high part.

SICILY. Some full-flavoured red and white table wines are produced, including the Corvo di Casteldaccia, the Faro and the Etna wines. The Mascato, Zucco and Albanello are of high alcoholic content. (*See also Marsala.*)

SHERRY. Wine made from white grapes in the Jerez district of southern Spain, fortified with Brandy. (*For varieties see page 108.*)

SOLERA. A basic wine of quality used in the blending of Sherries.

SOUTH AFRICA. Many red and white wines produced in the Cape Province and elsewhere are gaining in quality and in public recognition. The best wines come from Constantia, Paarl and Stellenbosch.

SOUTIRAGE. The process of racking a wine by drawing it off from the lees or deposit into another vat or cask.

SPÄTLESE. Refers to wines made from the last gathering of the ripest grapes from which fine German wines are made.

SPRITZIG. The very faint "prickle of fermentation" that can be detected in a young, still Moselle.

STREGA. A well-known Italian liqueur.

SUCCEEDED. Used when wine has developed the qualities expected of it.

SWITZERLAND. The most important wines come from the canton of Valais. Cortaillod is a red wine from Neuchâtel, Dezaley a white wine from the canton of Vaud.

SYLVANER. Originally an Austrian grape-vine, it is now second in quality only to the famous Riesling in the Rhineland vineyards.

TABLE WINE. A natural (i.e., unfortified) wine, red or white, suitable for drinking with food or to quench thirst.

TANNIN. An important natural element in red wine, derived from grape-pips, etc., giving it balance and firmness; but an excess of tannin creates astringency and delays the maturing processes.

TAPPIT HEN. The term, describing in Scotland a crested hen, was applied to a large pewter pot with a hen's head on the lid, holding three Imperial quarts. The term has sometimes been used to indicate a large bottle of Claret containing this quantity.

TARRAGONA. This cheap, strong red wine of the Port type was once more popular in Britain than it is today; it has to a great extent been displaced by heavy red wine manufactured in Britain.

TAVEL. From vineyards on the Rhône, this *vin rosé* is probably the best wine of its type now imported into Britain.

TAWNY PORT. Port which has matured in cask and acquired a tawny-red colour.

TODDY. Hot spirits with sugar and a little lemon. In Scotland there are (or were) special glasses called toddy-rummers in which potent Whisky-toddy was served.

TOKAY. This small village in North-east Hungary gives its name to a famous wine. The sweet concentrated *Tokaij Essencia* of great longevity is the best of the liqueur type. There are various grades of drier table wines.

TOM COLLINS. A long American drink composed of Gin, lime- or lemon-juice and a little sugar shaken up with ice; but there are various kinds, some with Brandy, some with Whisky as the base.

TONNEAU. A barrel containing 200 gal.

TROCKEN-BEEREN-AUSLESE. Individually picked overripe grapes from which the finest German wines are made.

TUN. A large cask containing 210 Imperial gal.

ULLAGE. In France the word *ouillage* means the filling up of a cask of which some of the contents have evaporated or been otherwise lost. In England, ullage refers to a bottle or cask no longer quite full—in the case of a bottle this being a fault due to a bad cork. A slightly ullaged bottle of Champagne might show little, if any, deterioration, but there would be serious deterioration with a Burgundy or Claret.

VALAIS. A canton in Switzerland that produces some of the best Swiss wines.

VAN DER HUM. A South African liqueur made with local Brandy flavoured with fruits and herbs.

VAT. A wine tub, large or small, traditionally made of oak, but sometimes nowadays made of concrete lined with glass, used both for fermentation and large-scale blending purposes.

VERMOUTH. A fortified white wine made near the Alpine regions of France and Italy, the Italian variety being deeper in colour and sweeter than the French.

VINO DE PASTO. Spanish for a table - wine; in Portuguese *Vinhos do Pasto.*

VINOSITY. The essential nature of wine which, properly speaking, is a concentration of the good qualities of its particular type. The word is sometimes used to refer only to alcoholic strength.

VINTAGE. The word for the harvesting of grapes has come to have a wide application, from the making of wine generally to the particular year in which a wine was made.

VODKA. A raw, immature spirit distilled in Russia, the "correct" way to drink it being to swallow it at a gulp.

VOUVRAY. A district in the Côteaux de Touraine, above Anjou, in the Loire valley, where both still and sparkling wines are made.

V.S.O. Very Special Old, referring to Brandy. V.S.O.P. means Very Special Old Pale. There is no guarantee that, in every case, Brandies so labelled are of any particular age.

WEEPER. A name given to a bottle with a leaky cork.

WHISKY. Scotch, Irish and American (Bourbon and Rye) are the principal kinds, each with its own characteristics that derive from the malting and fermenting of the different grains that form the bases, the distilling, maturing and blending, and the particular quality of the water used. The Irish and American spelling is *Whiskey.*

YUGOSLAVIA. Among pleasant beverage wines, the dry types are the Riesling, the Sylvaner and the Sauvignon, named after the grapes from which they were made. (*See also Maraschino.*)

INDEX

*For many names and terms not included in the Index
the reader is referred to the Wine Dictionary on page 142*